# Promoting fundamental British Values in the Early Years

**A guide to the Prevent duty and meeting the expectations of the new Common Inspection Framework**

by Marianne Sargent

## Contents

# Dedication

This is for my son Harry.
I hope you grow up in a world that supports the values promoted in this book.

# Acknowledgements

Grateful thanks to the early years settings that agreed to offer case study examples for this book; Positive Steps Nursery, Guildford, Mills Hill Primary School, Oldham, Horton Grange Primary School, Bradford, Parklands Nursery School, Northampton, Reflections Nursery & Forest School, Worthing.

Published by Practical Pre-School Books, A Division of MA Education Ltd, St Jude's Church, Dulwich Road, Herne Hill, London, SE24 0PB.

Tel: 020 7738 5454 www.practicalpreschoolbooks.com

© MA Education Ltd 2016

Design: Alison Coombes fonthillcreative 01722 717043

All images © MA Education with the exception of page 25 © Marianne Sargent

ISBN 978-1-909280-95-3

# Introduction

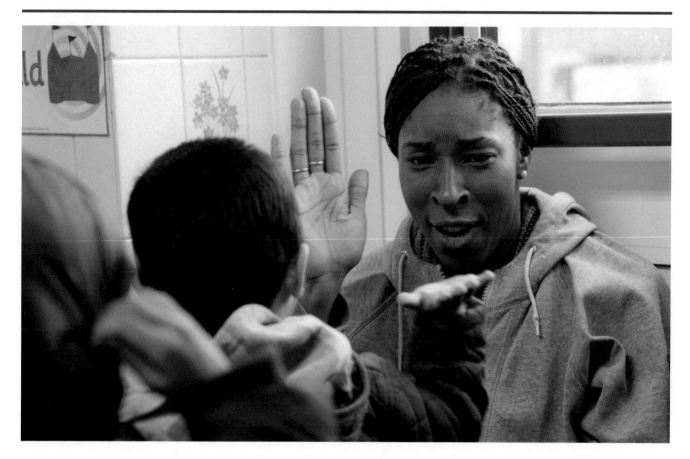

## About this book

This book is intended for early years professionals, trainers, students, leaders and nursery managers, and has been written in response to the increased focus over the past two years on actively promoting fundamental British values in education and childcare settings.

The recent introduction of the Common Inspection Framework (Ofsted, 2015a) has had significant implications for early years providers, which are now expected to produce evidence that they have robust safeguarding procedures and are actively promoting British values within their settings. The book aims to summarise the background to the Government's counter terrorism strategy Prevent, outline the associated legal responsibilities of early years providers, and explain the implications this has for safeguarding, child protection and curriculum delivery. It also takes an in-depth look at what the Government means by 'fundamental British values' and how these are implicit with the themes and principles of early years curricula in England, Scotland and Wales.

The main body of the book is divided into four parts, representing the four British values; democracy, rule of law, individual liberty, and mutual respect and tolerance

of different faiths and beliefs. Each value is considered in relation to the principles that underpin it and how these apply to the youngest members of British society. This is then supported with activity ideas linked to the Early Years Foundation Stage (EYFS) areas of learning and development, demonstrating how the curriculum presents many opportunities for exploring and promoting each of the British values. There are also illustrative case studies throughout, as well as 'Think about...' boxes containing questions that aid reflective practice.

At the end of the book there is a guide to inspection, which explains what Ofsted will be looking for in relation to providers' fulfilment of the Prevent duty. Here, there is also a table that explains what inspectors will do and what they will be looking for with advice about how to collect and provide evidence. Finally, there is a helpful checklist that aims to sum up the duty requirements at a glance.

The fact of the matter is that early years practitioners are already promoting British values during their everyday practice in the foundation stage setting. Therefore, this book aims to assist providers by pointing out where each of the values links to the curriculum and explaining what to evidence and highlight for inspection.

# The Prevent duty

Prevent is part of the UK Government's counter-terrorism strategy. It aims to target the 'extremist ideology at the heart' of terrorism by putting policies and programmes into place that will:

- 'respond to the **ideological challenge** of terrorism and the threat we face from those who promote it

- **prevent people from being drawn into terrorism** and ensure that they are given appropriate advice and support

- work with **sectors and institutions** where there are risks of radicalisation which we need to address.'
  (HM Government, 2011, pp.1 & 7)

As part of this aim the Counter-Terrorism and Security Act 2015 places a duty on 'specified authorities' in England, Scotland and Wales, including schools, nurseries, pre-schools, childminders and day care providers, **'to have due regard to the need to prevent people from being drawn into terrorism'**. This is described as the Prevent duty.

According to The Prevent strategy this means protecting children against extremist and violent views in the same way they are safeguarded from any other type of harm.

**'The purpose must be to protect children from harm and to ensure that they are taught in a way that is consistent with the law and our values.'** (HM Government, 2011, p.69).

There are two main areas of responsibility identified here:

1. Protecting children from harm by assessing and identifying their risk of being drawn into radicalisation.

2. Providing a safe, inclusive learning environment that supports spiritual, moral, social and cultural development through the promotion of fundamental British values.

## 1. Protecting children from harm

The Government states, 'early years providers serve arguably the most vulnerable and impressionable members of society' and 'must take action to protect children from harm and should be alert to harmful behaviour by other adults in the child's life' (HM Government, 2015a, p.10).

To help schools, nurseries and childcare providers understand their responsibilities in terms of protecting children from extremist and radicalised views the Government has produced a range of guidance materials.

The *Revised Prevent Duty Guidance for England and Wales* states **early years providers 'are subject to the duty to have due regard to the need to prevent people from being drawn into terrorism'** (HM Government, 2015a, p.10). *Working Together to Safeguard Children* (HM Government, 2015b) sets out the statutory safeguarding requirements as stipulated in the 1989 and 2004 Children Acts. *Keeping Children Safe in Education* (DfE, 2015a) further explains safeguarding procedures in educational settings.

**Early years professionals that work with young children in England should read all three documents in conjunction with each other**. Professionals in Wales should refer to the supporting guidance *Keeping Learners Safe* (Welsh Government, 2015).

The documents explain in order to fulfil the Prevent duty providers are expected to:

- Assess the risk of children being exposed to extremist ideas that are part of a terrorist ideology by being alert to any safeguarding issues in the child's life at home or elsewhere, and based on an understanding of the potential risk in the local area.

- Share information with other agencies to enable effective inter-agency assessment of the needs of individual children and ensure the appropriate intervention is put in place to prevent escalation.

- Have robust safeguarding policies to identify children at risk and intervene as appropriate. Settings are not required to write a separate Prevent policy, they just need to ensure the risk of radicalisation is included in existing safeguarding and child protection policies.

- Have a designated safeguarding lead to support practitioners and liaise with other agencies, and ensure all staff are aware of safeguarding procedures and the setting's child protection policy.

- Ensure safeguarding arrangements take into account the policies and procedures of the Local Safeguarding Children Boards in England, Local Service Boards in Wales and Child Protection Committees in Scotland.

- Ensure that staff receive training that enables them to more confidently identify children at risk of being drawn into terrorism, challenge extremist ideas and know where and how to refer children they feel are at risk.

- Provide a safe learning environment.

- Ensure children are not exposed to extremist material on the internet.

## More help and guidance

If you are concerned that a child is being exposed to extremist views and it is possible that they are at risk of being drawn into an environment that supports a terrorist ideology, or if you are unsure about whether you need to report something or not, you can get further advice from the following:

- *Statutory Framework for the Early Years Foundation Stage* (DfE, 2014a): Section 3 of this document sets out what early years practitioners are legally expected to do in terms of safeguarding and welfare requirements.

- *What do do if you're worried a child is being abused* (HM Government, 2015c): This publication provides practical guidance on understanding, identifying and reporting child abuse.

- *Information Sharing: Advice for practitioners providing safeguarding services to children* (HM Government, 2015d): This is a comprehensive guide which gives advice about how information should be recorded, stored and shared. It also provides a clear explanation as to when and how information should be shared.

- *The Prevent duty: Departmental advice for schools and*

*childcare providers* (DfE, 2015b): This clearly explains what is expected from schools and childcare providers in relation to identifying children at risk of radicalisation.

● *Channel Duty Guidance* (HM Government, 2015e): The Channel programme has been set up to provide a mechanism for schools to make referrals if they are concerned about the wellbeing of a child in terms of risk of radicalisation. This guidance explains why some people are drawn into terrorism and describes possible indicators.

● The Channel guidance includes a *Vulnerability Assessment Framework* (HM Government, 2012), which offers advice on how to assess whether someone is engaged with an extremist group or ideology, intent on causing harm and whether they have the capability to cause harm. In addition, there is an **online Channel training module**, which has been developed for front-line workers. This explains what Channel is and trains practitioners to identify risk factors with examples of appropriate types of intervention strategies. (http://course.ncalt.com/Channel_General_Awareness/01/index.html)

● Professionals in Scotland should refer to the *Revised Prevent Duty Guidance for Scotland* (HM Government, 2015f). There is also comprehensive guidance and advice on the Education Scotland website (www.educationscotland.gov.uk/readyforemergencies/terrorism/prevent/whatis.asp).

# 2. Promoting fundamental British values

This is the focus of this book. The Government suggests 'terrorism is associated with rejection of a cohesive, integrated, multi-faith society and of parliamentary democracy'. **It believes the prevention of radicalisation is 'dependent on developing a sense of belonging to this country and a support for our core values'** (HM Government, 2011, p.13). The Prevent strategy refers to these as 'fundamental British values' and defines them as:

● Democracy

● The rule of law

● Individual liberty

● Mutual respect and tolerance of different faiths and beliefs

The Prevent duty guidance states **schools and early years providers have a responsibility to actively promote**

**these fundamental British values** and the Department for Education (DfE, 2014b) has produced guidance for schools about how they can do this. The guidance, which is applicable to everyone who works with children of any age, explains staff should:

● Challenge opinions or behaviours that are contrary to British values.

● Enable children to develop their self-knowledge, self-esteem and self-confidence.

● Enable children to distinguish right from wrong and to respect the law.

● Encourage children to accept responsibility for their behaviour.

● Help children to understand how they can make a positive contribution to society.

● Help children to acquire a broad general knowledge of and respect for public services and institutions.

● Enable children to acquire an appreciation of and respect for their own and other cultures and traditions.

● Encourage children to respect others.

- Encourage children to respect democracy and the basis upon which the law is made and applied.

Educational Charity 4Children (2016) has also produced guidance for early years practitioners through its Foundation Years website, including the following examples of what is unacceptable:

- Actively promoting intolerance of other faiths, cultures and races.

- Failing to challenge gender stereotypes and routinely segregating sexes.

- Isolating children from their wider community.

- Failing to challenge behaviours that are contrary to British values.

**This book focuses on the promotion of fundamental British values in the early years setting. It looks in turn at democracy, the rule of law, individual liberty, and mutual respect and tolerance of different faiths and beliefs, and considers how they already are and can be promoted through early education in England, Wales and Scotland.**

# Defining 'fundamental British values'

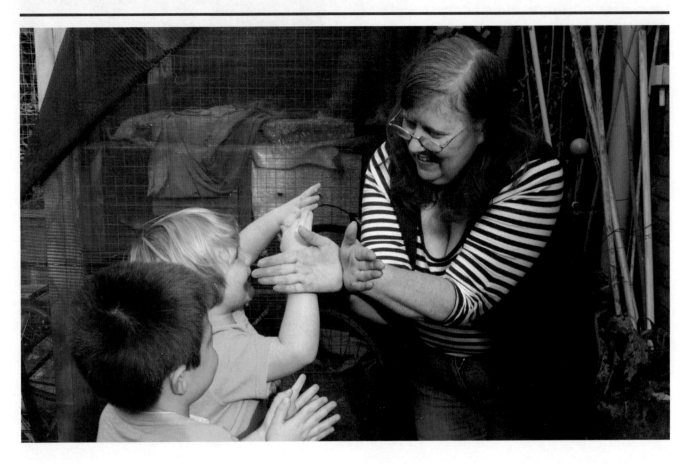

When the Government first announced its intention to make it a legal requirement that educational establishments actively promote British values, the inclusion of the word 'British' caused much controversy. In a letter to the education secretary Children's Laureate Michael Rosen explains why he finds the inclusion of the word 'British' so problematic:

> *'Your checklist of British values is: "Democracy, the rule of law, individual liberty, mutual respect, and tolerance of those of different faiths and beliefs." I can't attach the adjective "British" to these. In fact, I find it parochial, patronising and arrogant that you think it's appropriate or right to do so... We use adjectives to describe, modify, define, colour and infuse the noun that follows it. It's clear... that your government would like us to think that there is indeed something specially British about the items on the checklist.'* (Rosen, 2014)

Rosen takes issue with attaching the word 'British' to these particular values in a way that insinuates they are specific to any one nationality. It might also be argued that the use of the term 'British values' is contrary to the values of mutual tolerance and respect because identifying such values as 'British' sets them apart from the values of other societies and cultures around the world. The term might be construed as divisive rather than inclusive, ironically undermining the intention to promote community cohesion. Such values are equally applicable to people all over the world and as Goddard (2016) points out, many feel it is more appropriate to consider them as 'human' values.

Ofsted inspector Julia Gouldsboro, on the other hand, supports the use of the term 'British' and suggests 'having a more inclusive definition' of the word. An Irish immigrant, she draws on her own experience of growing up in England while struggling with her twin identity as an Irish national. She suggests societal division is resultant of a lack of 'sense of belonging' and 'generations still growing up with hatred for others because of their ethnicity':

> *'Britain is made up of small individual groups with many various cultures, races and religions, and we need*

*some umbrella to stand under that gives us an identity together... By British values, we do mean basic human values, but we need these to celebrate and proclaim that our diversity is actually our strongest bond and defines our "Britishness".'* (Gouldsboro, 2015, pp.49-50)

The inclusion of the word 'British' has also led to the misconception that promoting British values is about waving Union Jack flags, celebrating the English roast and sharing the stories of Beatrix Potter. Doing so is entirely missing the point. **Promoting British values is not about celebrating stereotypical British traditions and institutions, it is about encouraging the people of Britain to share a set of values that promote tolerance, respect and community cohesion**.

Many of the issues surrounding the term 'British values' and indeed the values identified are subject to debate. However, for the purposes of this book, the term is used throughout to avoid confusion.

# British values, human rights and human responsibilities

British early years settings should already be actively promoting the values of democracy, rule of law, individual liberty, and mutual tolerance and respect, as these are all represented within the Human Rights Act 1998 and United Nations Convention of the Rights of the Child (UNCRC) 1989. UNICEF's (2016) child-friendly explanation of the UNCRC mentions the importance of regarding these rights in relation to their associated responsibilities.

Therefore, when thinking about how to define each of the four British values it is helpful to consider how they promote human rights legislation because **introducing British values to young children is just the same as introducing them to their human rights and responsibilities**.

**Democracy:** A democracy is governed by representatives elected by the people. Ideally, its citizens should have equal rights, be treated fairly and be able to participate in decision making. Children's democratic rights are ratified by the UNCRC. Children have the right to participate in making decisions about things that concern them (article 12), they have the right to information (article 13), and they have a right to education and should be encouraged to strive to meet their full potential (article 28).

**The rule of law:** This is an understanding that a democratic society can only succeed if citizens abide by the rules. People who live in a law-abiding society are able to distinguish right from wrong and understand the consequences of their actions in terms of how they impact upon other individuals and society as a whole. The UNCRC

stipulates that children have the right to think what they want (article 14) and the right to freedom of association and peaceful assembly (article 15). However, they also have a responsibility to ensure that while enjoying these rights they do not stop others enjoying theirs.

**Individual liberty:** This is the freedom to make choices and voice opinions without fear of oppression. It means having freedom of expression in terms of choosing and portraying a personal identity and being able to express a personal point of view, which may be in opposition to others. It means having self-awareness and a positive sense of self. The UNCRC supports children's rights to think and believe what they want and to choose their own religion (article 14). It states education should promote children's individual personalities, talents and abilities and help them develop self-respect in terms of their family and cultural identity (article 29). UNICEF points out that with these rights come a responsibility to treat others with fairness and respect.

**Mutual respect and tolerance:** This is the expectation that people of different races, with different faiths, from varying cultural backgrounds and with opposing views and beliefs should be able to live and work together in peace. It means helping children learn about similarities and differences between people, teaching them to respect the views and beliefs of others and helping them appreciate why they should not discriminate against anyone on any basis. Again, this is covered in the UNCRC where it states education should promote respect for human rights and fundamental freedoms, as well as teach children to respect their own and other cultures, support sexual equality and demonstrate tolerance for people of different ethnicities and religions (article 29).

Article 4 of the Convention explains, 'States Parties shall undertake all appropriate legislative, administrative, and other measures for the implementation of the rights recognised in the present Convention' (UN, 1989). Governments are responsible for ensuring anyone caring for or working with children promotes their human rights. In this case the UK Government is upholding these rights by asking educators to actively promote British values.

# Fundamental British values and the EYFS

As well as being integral to human rights law, British values are embedded into UK education legislation. The Prevent duty guidance reiterates the legal responsibility of all schools and nurseries under the Education Act 2002 to **deliver a 'broad and balanced curriculum which promotes the spiritual, moral, cultural, mental and physical development of pupils and prepares them for the opportunities, responsibilities and experiences of later life'** (HM Government, 2015a, p.10). The guidance also refers to the Education and Inspections Act 2006, which highlights the duty of the school inspectorate to report upon **'the contribution made by the school to community cohesion'**.

Promoting British values is about more than activities and resources. Managers and leaders must ensure British values are promoted through the ethos of the setting and its policies and procedures. Most helpfully, these values **are implicit within the themes and principles of the Statutory Framework for the Early Years Foundation Stage**.

## A unique child

The EYFS states, 'every child is a unique child who is constantly learning and can be resilient, capable, confident and self-assured' (DfE, 2014a, p.6). The underlying principle here is that individual children should be respected and have access to early years provision that fosters their unique aptitudes and abilities and enables them to thrive and develop. This means planning a curriculum that reflects the diversity of children's interests and experiences and caters for their differing needs. What's more, there is an expectation that all children and their families will be respected and valued and not be discriminated against on any basis.

This means creating a democratic environment where all children are treated fairly and parents are included and involved (democracy); children are respected as individuals and encouraged to express themselves freely (individual liberty); and all children, their parents and families are respected and catered for (mutual respect and tolerance).

## Positive relationships

This theme encompasses the principle that 'children learn to be strong and independent through positive relationships' (DfE, 2014a, p.6). Through the key person system children (and families) are able to develop secure attachments that will make them feel more confident and encourage them to become more independent. The Development Matters guidance explains positive relationships should 'foster a sense of belonging' and be 'responsive to the child's needs, feelings and interests' (Early Education, 2012, p.2).

This means supporting children to become independent and autonomous thinkers (individual liberty), while guiding and helping them to develop a sense of right and wrong so they are able to start regulating their own behaviour (rule of law). What's more, it means working hard to promote positive relationships with parents, respecting their role as the first educator and valuing their views and opinions (mutual respect and tolerance).

## Enabling Environments

'Children learn and develop well in enabling environments' (DfE, 2014a, p.6). The underlying principle here is that children

develop and make better progress in a learning environment that is responsive to their individual needs and interests. An enabling environment offers 'stimulating resources, relevant to all the children's cultures and communities' and provides rich playful learning opportunities (Early Education, 2012, p.2).

This means planning learning experiences around the needs and interests of the different children in the setting (democracy). Children should experience a supportive environment where they are not afraid to take risks and failure is seen as a positive part of the learning journey (individual liberty). Practitioners should teach children the benefits of working together to solve problems and meet goals (democracy) and children should be helped to understand how their behaviour can have a positive or negative affect on themselves and others (rule of law). Furthermore, practitioners should value diversity in terms of how it benefits all who attend the setting (mutual respect and tolerance).

## Learning and development

This theme encompasses the principle that 'children develop and learn in different ways and at different rates' (DfE, 2014a, p.6). Individual children will have a range of aptitudes and abilities that reflect a variety of interests and strengths in different areas of learning. Children in the early years learn in a variety of ways; through independent exploration and play, as well as carefully planned adult-led focused activities. The curriculum is delivered with three characteristics of effective learning in mind: playing and exploring, active learning, and creating and thinking critically.

The EYFS is a democratic curriculum that acknowledges the difference between individual children and the way they learn. Observation is central to early years practice and and is used to inform planning so that provision meets the needs and interests of individual children (democracy). The EYFS gives children the freedom to play, explore and learn in their own way and encourages them to find out for themselves (individual liberty). It aims to motivate children to have a go, persist in their efforts and celebrate their achievements, as well as to manage their feelings and behaviour when things do not turn out as planned (individual liberty, rule of law). What's more, it encourages children to have their own ideas, make their own choices and express their own opinions (democracy, individual liberty, mutual respect and tolerance).

As well as being implicit in the themes and principles of the EYFS, British values are also woven into the fabric of the curriculum:

> *'Early years providers already focus on children's personal, social and emotional development. The Early Years Foundation Stage framework supports early years*

flourish in life, learning and work, now and in the future, and to appreciate their place in the world' (Education Scotland, 2016). These four capacities – to become successful learners, confident individuals, responsible citizens and effective contributors – support the principles that underpin all four British values.

**This book looks at how fundamental British values are reflected in the EYFS. However, all the case studies and activities are equally applicable to early years settings in Wales and Scotland.**

*providers to do this in an age appropriate way, through ensuring children learn right from wrong, mix and share with other children and value others' views, know about similarities and differences between themselves and others, and challenge negative attitudes and stereotypes.'* (HM Government, 2015a, p.10).

# Wales and Scotland

The Welsh Foundation Phase Framework (WFPF) upholds broadly the same principles as the EYFS with emphasis on planning for the individual needs of the developing child, delivering an inclusive learning programme and providing a stimulating environment that fosters active learning. However, the WFPF makes specific reference to the UNCRC and the responsibility of settings to 'develop in every child a sense of personal and cultural identity that is receptive and respectful towards others' and to 'plan across the curriculum to develop the knowledge and understanding, skills, values and attitudes that will enable children to participate in our multi-ethnic society in Wales' (DfES, 2015, p.5). British values are at its core.

The Scottish Curriculum for Excellence (SCE) aims to help children develop four capacities which 'aim to ensure that all children and young people in Scotland develop the knowledge, skills and attributes they will need if they are to

# For society but also for the individual

Although the main objective of the Prevent strategy is to promote a set of values that contribute toward creating a cohesive society, such values are of course beneficial to the development of the individual child. This can be illustrated by looking at how fundamental British values support the characteristics of effective learning identified in the EYFS.

## Playing and exploring

Young children learn through engaging with the world around them; actively exploring and playing. These experiences are more rewarding in a democratic learning environment where everyone is able to share, take turns and work cooperatively. Children also need to be able to follow rules and understand the difference between right and wrong if they are to successfully share the learning space. In addition, they will get more from their play experiences if they are encouraged to participate in decision making, including deciding what they would like to learn about and which resources they would like to have access to.

Children who are helped to develop self-confidence and exercise freedom of choice and expression will be able to take greater advantage of their learning environment. These children will be more willing to take risks and less afraid to make mistakes. They will also be more inquisitive and talkative, enabling them to make the most out of the learning opportunities put in front of them.

## Active learning

Children are motivated and engaged when they are interested, and the extent to which the learning environment reflects their interests is dependent upon whether their views, opinions and ideas are taken into account. A democratic setting will plan around the fascinations, needs, aptitudes and abilities of the children. They will be encouraged to question, debate and investigate despite the risk of failure and their achievements will be celebrated, helping them develop a sense of individual worth.

# Creating and thinking critically

Like the others this characteristic is underpinned by the values of democracy and individual liberty. Creative and critical thinking is all about children thinking for themselves, voicing their opinions and having their own ideas. It involves encouraging them to be independent learners; to make predictions, try things out and decide how to approach tasks and solve problems.

However, for children to move on in their learning they also need to be able to work and play cooperatively and collaboratively. Thinking evolves when we share our ideas and have them challenged and extended by more knowledgable adults and peers. Children who have good communication skills and the ability to work harmoniously with others will have greater opportunity to extend their thinking and develop their knowledge. This demonstrates the importance of being able to regulate behaviour and respect others.

As well as benefitting society as a whole, these lifelong learning skills will assist the individual child throughout their learning career and help improve their individual prospects.

# Democracy

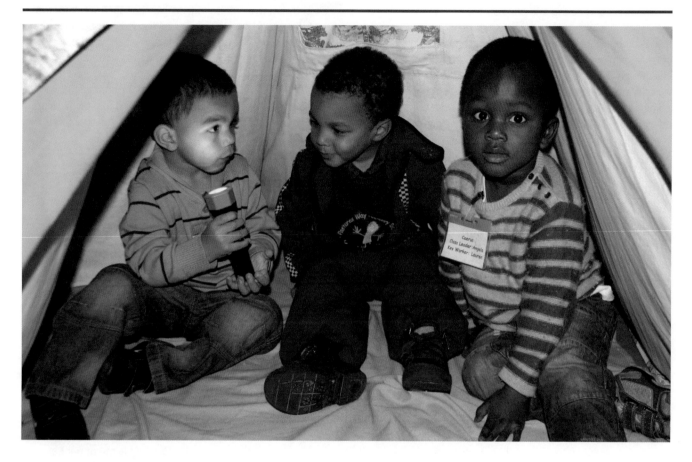

The people of Britain live within a democracy. The ideals of democracy promote a shared belief in fairness and equality and a right to participate in important decision making. Arising from these ideals is an emphasis on shared responsibility, mutual respect and the wider community. When considering how to teach children about democracy in the early years it is helpful to think about these underlying democratic principles and how they relate to the issues and concerns of young children.

**Fairness and equality:** In the early years this involves helping children to understand that sharing, taking turns and working and playing cooperatively contributes to a fairer society.

**Participation:** With young children this means encouraging them to share their views and opinions, involving them in decision making processes and encouraging ollaborative activity.

**Shared responsibility:** Children should be taught to respect each other and work together to create a positive learning community. This means helping them form positive relationships with each other.

It is possible to promote democracy and explore the ideas that underpin it through the following EYFS areas of learning and development.

## Personal, social and emotional development

The EYFS supports democratic thinking through the making relationships strand of personal, social and emotional development. Here children are taught the benefits of developing positive relationships that support fair play and cooperation, as well as the value of participating and working collaboratively.

## Fairness and equality

A big challenge for young children is learning to share time, space and resources with others. One of the most effective ways to help children develop these skills is to play plenty of games that involve turn taking. For example:

- Establish the basic rules of turn taking with conversation and by using activities, board and card games such as snakes and ladders, lotto, matching pairs, snap, four in a row, noughts and crosses and happy families.

- Circle games where children take turns to speak, for example, the alphabet game, I spy, name clap, Chinese whispers and my favourite things.

# Democracy

- Parachute games such as sharks, all change, Mexican wave, parachute tag and shoe shuffle.

It is also important to model fair treatment by ensuring all children within the setting have equal opportunities. Young children have a very acute sense of what is fair and what is not and in the early years it is very common to hear the phrase 'It's not fair'. Help them understand what constitutes as fair and equal treatment in the following ways:

- Choose register monitors on a weekly basis. Display a list showing who will be register monitor each week for the term and tick off the names as the weeks pass by. Refer to the list at the beginning of each week when pointing out whose turn it is.

- Put children's names on tiny slips of paper inside balloons and pin them somewhere reasonably high up. Pop a balloon each morning to select your personal

## Personal, social and emotional development

| Aspect | Development statement/ Early Learning Goal | How does this link to democracy? | Practice that promotes democracy |
|---|---|---|---|
| **Making relationships**<br><br>**Managing feelings and behaviour** | Plays co-operatively, taking turns with others.<br><br>Begins to accept the needs of others and can take turns and share resources, sometimes with support from others. | Within a democracy everyone should be treated fairly and have equal rights. | Helping children understand the need to take turns in their play and allow each other's ideas to lead play themes.<br><br>Teaching children the importance of sharing resources so everyone has an equal opportunity to learn and play.<br><br>Modelling fair treatment by ensuring equal opportunities for all children in the setting. |
| **Making relationships**<br><br><br><br><br><br><br>**Managing feelings and behaviour** | Takes account of one another's ideas about how to organise their activity.<br><br>Shows sensitivity to others' needs and feelings and forms positive relationships with adults and other children.<br><br>Beginning to be able to negotiate and solve problems without aggression, e.g. when someone has taken their toy. | Within a democracy everyone should have the right to participate and have their views considered.<br><br>A democratic community is forged through positive relationships and working together. | Encouraging children to take account of each other's ideas when they are playing and working together.<br><br>Involving children in planning topics, themes and activities.<br><br>Involving children in decision making.<br><br>Exploring feelings with the children and helping them to empathise with others.<br><br>Mediating when children have disagreements and helping them to suggest solutions and come up with ideas for how they can resolve differences.<br><br>Teaching children the importance of shared responsibility by encouraging them to all take an active role in looking after each other and the learning environment. |

## Case study: Learning to share

Thomas and Archie (age 4) are playing with a Hot Wheels track. Thomas has built a loop-the-loop and believes only one car is capable of successfully travelling around it without falling off. Archie is playing with that particular car and does not want to let Thomas use it for the same reason. A practitioner approaches and asks if the boys have any ideas how they can make a fair decision as to who can play with the car. Thomas suggests they take turns with the car and and each have equal amounts of time to play with it. Archie agrees. The practitioner praises Thomas' good idea and suggests using a five-minute sand timer so they can each see when their time is up.

In this example, the boys were given the chance to make suggestions as to how to solve the problem themselves. Thomas came up with an idea that was fair and the practitioner supported this by suggesting the use of a sand timer, enabling the boys to monitor their own practice of fair and equal treatment independently.

## Case study: Early years democracy

Positive Steps Nursery in Guildford caters for children aged three months to five years and the children are divided into four rooms according to age. One child is chosen to represent each room on a children's council that meets once a week. The council talks about what everyone has been learning and how this can be extended and developed into projects that further extend the children's needs and interests.

The children are encouraged to talk about what they enjoy doing and which aspects of the learning environment they find most stimulating. They are then invited to suggest changes and come up with their own ideas for activities. For example, one pre-school child said she enjoyed collecting objects and would like to go out on walks to collect things. So staff planned some walks off-site and while the children were out they came across a bus stop. This triggered an interest in public transport and eventually lead to a project that involved taking rides on the bus and train.

Even babies and very young children participate on the council. They are accompanied to meetings by their key workers, who share observations and talk about the children's interests on their behalf. For example, observations of a baby who particularly enjoyed messy play but also being outside led to staff setting up more messy play in the outdoor area.

This demonstrates how children can be democratically involved in planning and making decisions about their own learning. It is a great example of child-centred practice.

assistant for the day. Throw the slip of paper in the bin and point out it will be someone else's turn tomorrow.

- Send a setting mascot home with a different child each weekend. Again, keep a list and tick off the names. Arrange this list so the children who are last on the register list go first on this list.

## Participation

Perhaps the most straightforward way to enable children to actively participate is to ask them what they want to learn and involve them in topic planning. This is already integral to many early years practitioners' practice and recognised as a good example of starting from the child.

## Involving children in decision making

Another way to include children in decision making processes, is the creation of a children's council:

- Once every six weeks bring the children together in their key worker groups and show them how to elect a representative for a children's council.

- Bring the council together once a week to consider important issues such as:
  - Suggestions for healthy snack choices
  - Ideas for role play area themes

- Play resources that the children would like provided indoors and outside
- Activities the children have enjoyed
- Ideas for extending activities
- Additions or alterations to the setting code

## Shared responsibility

Part of being in a democracy means working together to improve outcomes for all. In the early years setting this means helping children to form positive relationships and fostering a collaborative culture where everyone helps each other out. Practitioners should encourage children to respect each other and consider the needs and feelings of others. It is also helpful to mediate when children have disagreements and encourage them to compromise and come up with their own solutions.

## Case study: Helping each other

It is tidy up time and Helen (age 3) is in charge of sweeping up the sand area with Adrian (age 3). Adrian immediately picks up a dustpan and brush and starts to sweep. Helen plays in the sand. The nursery lead approaches Helen and asks why she is not helping Adrian. Helen shrugs. The practitioner asks Helen if she thinks it is fair to let Adrian do all the work. She shrugs again.

The practitioner notices that Adrian has completed half the sweeping. She asks Adrian if he thinks it is fair that he should do the whole job alone. Adrian shakes his head emphatically and says 'No!' The practitioner asks Helen if she thinks it is fair. Helen shrugs and says 'No'. The practitioner asks Helen what she thinks she can do about it. Helen picks up a dustpan and starts to sweep.

Here, instead of simply telling Helen to pick up a dustpan and start sweeping, the nursery lead asks Helen to consider the consequences of her actions. She prompts Helen to think about whether her behaviour is fair and how it is affecting Adrian.

## Encouraging children to take responsibility

It is also a good idea to get children actively involved in caring for their learning environment and one way to do this is through the use of a task board.

Set up a task board with care-taking jobs on it, for example, sweeping up the sand, washing the paint pots, clearing up the writing table, tidying up the book corner and hanging up the water aprons. Stick laminated photos of the children on one side of the board.

### Think about...
...how you promote equality and fairness, involve the children in decision making, invite their participation and encourage them to take responsibility:

- Are the children given the chance to think about what is fair and why?

- Do you seek their opinions about what they want to learn and what they want to do?

- How do you ensure everyone's views are respected and given equal consideration?

- How do you encourage everyone to work together and take responsibility for looking after each other and the learning environment?

Each morning move two photos next to each task to show which children are responsible for that task for the day. At the end of the day move the photos off the board and stick them on the opposite side to indicate they have done a job already. Then the following day stick two new photos next to each job. Throughout the week encourage children to independently check the board to see if they are responsible for anything in particular. When all the children have had a turn, move all the photos back to the start.

# Physical development

Sports and team games present opportunities for illustrating the concepts of fair play and democratic decision making, as well as the benefits of team work and cooperation.

## Physical development

| Aspect | Development statement/ Early Learning Goal | How can you use physical development to help explore democratic principles? |
|---|---|---|
| **Moving and handling** | Negotiates space successfully when playing racing and chasing games with other children, adjusting speed or changing direction to avoid obstacles; shows increasing control over an object in throwing, catching or kicking it. | Play games that involve children sharing space and watching out for each other.<br><br>Play games that involve taking turns and sharing equipment.<br><br>Play team games that involve team work and cooperation. |

## Fair play

The following sports and physical activities help children learn to take turns, play fair, cooperate and negotiate rules.

- Playground games such as hop scotch, duck duck goose, hide and seek, and cat and mouse.

- Sports that require children to share equipment like football, basketball, tennis, hockey and skittles.

- Relay races that encourage children to cheer each other on and work together as a team.

- Movement games that require children to share and negotiate space such as traffic lights, cat and mouse and capture the flag.

## Team work and cooperation

Illustrate the power of active participation and collaboration by getting the children to work together whilst playing some team games. Try the following:

- Stuck in the mud: Select five chasers, everyone else should run away. The chasers must catch up to and tap runners on the arm. When tapped, runners must stand still with legs apart and arms out as if stuck. Other runners can free them by crawling between their legs. The game is over once all the runners have been captured and are stuck.

- Balloon smash: Five children stand on each side of a dividing line across the middle of a large space. An adult throws a balloon in the air. The children must hit the balloon over the line towards the opposing team. The balloon must not touch the floor. Each time the balloon touches the floor on one side of the line, the team on the opposite side gets a point. First team to 10 points wins.

- Five-a-side ball games: Any goal scoring game will work. Divide the children into two teams and see who can score the most goals in an allotted time.

## Literacy

Stories enable early years practitioners to introduce important issues to young children in an age-appropriate way. There is a wealth of picture books that explore ideas linked to democracy including those below as well as others listed in the resources section at the back of this book.

## The benefits of sharing

*Romp in the Swamp* by Ian Whybrow and Adrian Reynolds (Puffin) – in this story Harry does not want to share his dinosaurs when he visits a little girl called Charlie. However, Charlie manages to show him the benefits of sharing when she comes up with a great dinosaur play theme.

**Reflecting on the story: Why is it better to share and take turns?** Ask the children to consider what might have happened if Harry had continued to refuse to share. Would he still be happy with that decision by the end of the day? How would Charlie have felt? What might they both have done instead of playing together?

Use large puppets to present the children with a scenario that will start a discussion about sharing and taking turns. Set up and take a photo of two puppets playing side by side, one playing with a toy and the other with his head in his hands crying.

Show the photo to the children and ask them what they think has happened. Do they have any ideas about how the puppets might be able to solve the problem? Can they offer any ideas about sharing and playing fair?

## Literacy

| Aspect | Development statement/ Early Learning Goal | How can you use stories to help explore democratic principles? |
|---|---|---|
| **Reading** | Begins to be aware of the way stories are structured; suggests how the story might end; listens to stories with increasing attention and recall; describes main story settings, events and principal characters. | Introduce children to characters who are faced with issues related to fairness, equality, participation and shared responsibility.<br><br>Ask children to empathise with characters and think about why something might be unfair and how this can be remedied.<br><br>Ask them to consider the events in a story and how they are evolving. Can the children predict what might happen next and explain why? What will happen if the characters work together/play fair/share? What will happen if not? |
| **Reading** | Demonstrates understanding when talking with others about what they have read. | Ask children to explain what happened. Was everyone treated fairly? Did the characters work together? If so, what happened as a result? If not, what were the consequences?<br><br>Encourage children to reflect upon the characters and events in stories and consider them in relation to their own experiences. |

## Getting involved and working together

*The Giant Jam Sandwich* by John Vernon Lord and Janet Burroway (Red Fox) – this classic story is great for illustrating the benefits of collaborating and working together to solve a problem. A small village is besieged by wasps spurring villagers on to hatch a plan to get rid of them; a trap in the guise of a giant jam sandwich.

**Reflecting on the story: How can we work together?**
Ask the children if they can explain the message or moral of the story. Can they suggest what might have happened if the villagers had not worked together in the way that they did? What would have happened to the village and its residents? How did working together benefit everyone?

Help children to appreciate the benefits of working together by posing some problems and asking for their help with solving them. For example:

- The cloakroom area is in a terrible mess and things keep getting lost. Why is this happening? What can we do about it?

- People keep tripping over bits and pieces and models in the construction area. How can we solve this?

- Balls keep rolling through the railings and out into the playground. How can we stop this happening?

- The paint brushes have gone hard and we can't use them. What can we do to prevent this?

- Milk and water keep getting spilled on the floor in the snack area. What can we do to stop this happening?

Ask the children if they have any ideas about how these problems might be solved. Encourage them to think of ways they can take responsibility for putting the solutions into place. Allocate jobs and roles to volunteers. Get the children working in pairs and groups to put things into place.

## Looking after each other

*The Emperor's Egg* by Martin Jenkins and Jane Chapman (Walker Books) – a cross between a story book and information book, this tells about how emperor penguins raise their young. It explains the different roles of the mother and father penguins and how penguins huddle together during snow storms to keep each other warm.

**Reflecting on the story: How can we take care of each other?** Emperor penguins are a good example of how a society can work together for the greater good. The penguins look after each other so they are able to protect their eggs and raise their young safely. There are other examples of this in nature including bees and ants.

Visit a library and find out more about bees and ants. How do they live? What do they need to do to survive? Have any of the children ever watched a colony of ants working together? Help the children build an ant farm so they can observe the ants work together to dig tunnels and build a home.

Encourage the children to relate their knowledge of these minibeasts to their own experience. How can they ensure their setting is a nice place to be? How can they help others feel comfortable and happy? How can they work together to look after the toys and resources? How can they share responsibility for looking after each other and make sure everyone is able to learn?

# Mathematics

Mathematics presents a number of opportunities for illustrating the concept of fairness and democratic decision making, which is helpful when introducing the idea of equal opportunities and equal rights to younger children. Use number problems to explain what a fair share is and introduce the concept of a survey to identify a majority.

## A fair share

Use snack to demonstrate how everyone is entitled to a fair share. Set up a snack table for children to independently help themselves. Lay out name cards and a post box for the children to post their names when they go for snack. This will help you keep track of how many children have already had snack. Place the food on the table and put up a sign that shows how much food the children should take, for example, one orange and two crackers.

If the food runs out before everyone has visited the snack table, bring the children together and explain the food has run out because someone had more than their fair share. Steer the children away from naming and shaming but instead ask them what they think everyone should do next time. Then, of course, bring out the extra food you have kept aside for those children who have not yet eaten!

## Democratic decision making

Model democratic decision making by giving children options, surveying their responses and recording them graphically to show which is the most popular choice. It might be that you are planning a trip off-site and decide to ask the children where they would prefer to go, giving them options such as the play-park, beach or museum. Otherwise you may want to ask the children for their opinion as to how to set up the role play area or which construction should be made available for the day.

Present the survey visually by sticking a photo of each option (location, role play theme or construction kit) on a whiteboard, then ask the children to come out one at a time and put a tick next to their choice. You can then refer to the graph to show the children which option has the majority vote and is therefore the most popular choice.

## Mathematics

| Aspect | Development statement/ Early Learning Goal | How can you use mathematics to help explore democratic principles? |
|---|---|---|
| **Numbers** | Uses some language of quantities; solves problems, including sharing. | Teach children to share out quantities equally. |
| **Numbers** | Uses the language of 'more' and 'fewer' to compare sets of objects; records, using marks that they can interpret and explain. | Include the children in democratic decision making by surveying the group and going with the majority.* |

*There is also a link to the technology aspect of understanding the world here. When surveying children, displaying the results of surveys in the form of pictograms and graphs on the interactive whiteboard is a good way of visually explaining a majority vote (see also 'democratic decision making' above).

# Rule of law

British citizens are expected to abide by the rule of law. This means being able to follow rules, distinguish between right and wrong, and understand the consequences of negative and illegal actions in terms of how they impact upon other individuals and society as a whole.

This is a complex topic with a number of issues threading through it. There are various factors that impact upon an individual's understanding of right and wrong, influence their behaviour and compel them to care about consequences. Young children need to explore these issues if they are to grow into responsible adults who have a healthy respect for the law. Therefore, in the early years it is helpful to look at the relationship between feelings and behaviour, and behaviour and consequences.

**Feelings and behaviour:** Part of teaching about rule of law in the early years involves exploring feelings and thinking about how they impact upon behaviour. Children need to learn to understand how they feel and why. If they can do this they will be better able to manage their feelings and regulate their behaviour.

**Behaviour and consequences:** Children should be taught to think for themselves. It is not enough to tell them something is wrong and not to do it. They need to understand why. They should be encouraged to consider the consequences of their actions for themselves as well as to empathise with others and and think about how their actions affect those around them. It is a good idea to encourage young children to take ownership of the rules that govern them so they can better understand the reasons that underpin them. Also, allow them to question authority and invite them to engage in debate.

It is possible to promote the rule of law and explore the issues surrounding it through the following EYFS areas of learning and development.

## Personal, social and emotional development

In order to successfully function and thrive within a society people need to respect the rule of law. Personal, social and emotional development in the EYFS focuses on helping children to understand the need for rules, as well as the consequences for themselves and others when they break those rules.

# Personal, social and emotional development

| Aspect | Development statement/ Early Learning Goal | How does this link to the rule of law? | Practice that promotes the rule of law |
|---|---|---|---|
| **Managing feelings and behaviour** | Talks about how they and others show feelings, talks about their own and others' behaviour, and its consequences, and knows that some behaviour is unacceptable. | When laws are broken and rules are ignored there are consequences for all involved. | Exploring feelings with the children and finding out:<br><br>● How their feelings affect their behaviour;<br>● How they feel about the fairness of certain rules;<br>● How they feel about breaking the rules;<br>● How they feel about others breaking rules.<br><br>Exploring the difference between right and wrong. How do we know whether something is right or wrong?<br><br>Involving the children in deciding on appropriate sanctions when drawing up a behaviour code.[†] |
| **Managing feelings and behaviour** | Works as part of a group or class, and understands and follows the rules. | Abiding by laws and rules has a positive impact upon individual achievement and society as a whole. | Helping children understand the need for laws and rules.<br><br>Involving the children in drawing up a setting behaviour code.[†]<br><br>Establishing regular routines so children understand what is expected of them. |
| **Making relationships** | Plays co-operatively, taking turns with others.<br><br>Shows sensitivity to others' needs and feelings and forms positive relationships with adults and other children. | Laws and rules are created in order to ensure people can live together in peace and safety. | Helping children understand the importance of behaving in a way that is considerate of others.<br><br>Helping children to understand that unkind or thoughtless behaviours have a negative impact upon others. |
| **Self-confidence and self-awareness** | Confident to speak to others about own needs, wants, interests and opinions. | Respecting the rule of law involves questioning authority and government.* | Allowing children to question rules and inviting them to debate the issue.<br><br>Introducing children to a variety of opinions and viewpoints. |

[†]There are also links to democracy here. Democratic practice involves ensuring children are actively involved in important decision making processes.

*This is important because it also supports the values of democracy and individual liberty.

## Understanding feelings and behaviour

Wayland has produced a series of books by Brian Moses and Mike Gordon that deal with emotions and how they make people behave. The books have fantastic illustrations that really help to convey the emotions the characters are feeling. Titles including, *I Feel Angry* and *I Feel Jealous* and the more recent *Anna Angrysaurus* and *Jamal Jealousaurus* deal with negative emotions that prompt negative behaviours. In addition, titles including *I Feel Sad*, *It's Not Fair* and *Samuel Scaredosaurus* help children to empathise with how it feels to be sad, hard done by and afraid.

The characters in these books describe each feeling using imagery that young children will be able to understand and go on to explain how the feeling makes them behave, again with examples that children will easily identify with. The books are a very helpful starting point for exploring different feelings, how we deal with them and the consequences of letting them get the better of us, as well as for helping children empathise with the feelings of others.

Also well worth a look is a series of therapeutic stories by Jane Evans and Izzy Bean, published by Jessica Kingsley. These stories are aimed at helping children with social and emotional problems and include questions for children to aid reflection, as well as guidance for parents and professionals. *Little Meerkat's Big Panic* aims to help children manage feelings of

anxiety, stress and panic, while *Kit Kitten* and the *Topsy Turvy Feelings* and *How are You Feeling Today Little Bear?* aim to help children understand and manage the feelings associated with difficult life events and home circumstances.

## Exploring different emotions

Play a circle game that encourages children to explore and describe feelings. It is best to play this game with no more than five children at a time so they are only expected to sit and maintain attention for a short period.

Print a set of faces that express a range of feelings and place them in a feely bag (or see the emotion stones in the resources section at the back of this book). Sit in a circle and pass the bag and a mirror around to one child at a time. Each child takes a face out of the bag and describes the emotion in the facial expression. They then say, 'I feel… when…' and suggest something that makes them feel like the expression on the picture. They then make a face that portrays that particular feeling, using the mirror to help. When all the children have had a go ask if anyone can remember experiencing that feeling, why and what happened.

## Knowing where they stand

Young children thrive in a stable environment where they know where they are and what they are doing. Children who are unsure about what is expected of them will inevitably find it difficult to follow rules. This highlights the importance of establishing regular routines so children are able to follow the pattern of the day and keep in step with everyone else.

One way of making children aware of routines is to begin each day with a run-down of what will be happening. This may be done as a 'plan of the day' with a list of times alongside pictures of activities. Another way is to have a 'What's the time Mr Wolf?' display featuring a clock in the middle with movable hands, and photos around the edges next to corresponding times. Practitioners can revisit these displays throughout the day to look at what has happened and what is yet to come.

It is especially helpful to establish regular routines, whereby everyone tidies up together at the end of the morning and afternoon each day, equipment and toys are kept in clearly labeled places, everyone goes to the toilet and washes their hands before lunch, everyone lines up in certain places for particular activities and everyone puts their personal belongings in a particular place. Keeping things simple and repetitive will help children to follow rules and meet expectations. It will also help them to feel more secure so when the routine has to change for any reason, they will be better able to cope with it.

## Taking ownership

Rather than imposing rules on children, get them involved in devising a behaviour code and ask for their ideas about appropriate sanctions. This will help them to start considering the difference between right and wrong and why.

Puppets are so powerful when it comes to thinking about the consequences of breaking rules. Early years consultant Ros Bayley long advocated the use of puppets and toys to encourage discussion and thought among young children. Training with her some years ago inspired the following idea.

Consider the rules that you feel are important for your particular setting then take photos of puppets breaking those rules (this is picture 1). Think about the consequences of breaking each rule and take a photo of the puppet suffering those consequences (this is picture 2). For example:

● A puppet running through a classroom toward a train set that is laid out on the floor (1), then the puppet sprawled on the floor with the train scattered everywhere (2).

● A puppet climbing on the block trolley (1), then the puppet under a pile of bricks on the floor (2).

● A puppet pushing a friend (1), then the friend crying (2).

### Case study: Children learning to manage their own behaviour

Mills Hill Primary School in Oldham has adopted a brain-based approach to classroom management called 'conscious discipline' that aims to develop self-discipline within children so they are able to recognise for themselves what is expected rather than be told by someone else.

The approach begins in the nursery, where children learn the vocabulary they need to be able to settle minor conflicts so they are able to resolve them independently rather than seeking the help of a teacher. When the teacher does need to intervene however, the children are given positive choices. This means instead of telling children to do something or face a sanction, the teacher presents them with positive options that give them a choice about how they do something. For example, if a child is reluctant to tidy up some coloured bricks the teacher might ask, 'Do you want to put the red or blue blocks in the box first?'

Every classroom in the school also has a 'safe place' where children can go when they are feeling angry, upset or frustrated. In each safe place there are comforting objects and the children are taught strategies they can use to help themselves calm down, such as breathing exercises.

This is a positive example of an effective behaviour management strategy that supports children and helps them learn how to manage their own behaviour from a very early age.

● A group of puppets playing with a toy together (1), then the group with their hands in the air while one of the puppets is playing with the toy alone (2).

Bring the children together and explain you are going to show them some photos to help create a behaviour code for the setting. Show them a photo of a puppet breaking a rule (1) and ask:

● What do you think is happening in this picture?

● What do you think might happen next?

● Why do you think it is going to happen?

Then show the children the photo of the puppet suffering the consequences (2) and ask:

● Were we right about what we thought might happen?

● How do you think s/he feels?

- What should s/he have done instead?

- Do you think we might need a rule about this?

- What should that rule be?

Help the children to phrase the rule in a positive way, for example, rather than 'do not run indoors', state the rule as 'we walk indoors'. Look at each photo in turn to decide on the rest of the rules. Try not to make up too many and keep them simple.

Then ask the children to think about possible sanctions for breaking the rules. Suggest they consider sanctions that rectify and create solutions rather than punishments. For instance, the sanction for negligently knocking over someone's construction model when running indoors might be to help rebuild it.

Display the photos and the rules on a low level display or wall where the children can see them easily. Whenever a child is breaking a rule, take them to the display and ask them what happened when the puppet was breaking that same rule. This is an effective visual reminder of rules and possible consequences that the children can relate to and will remember.

---

### Think about...
...how you help children to understand their feelings, control and take ownership of their behaviour, and distinguish between right and wrong:

- How do you help children see the relationship between feelings, emotions and behaviour?

- How do you ensure children understand what is expected of them?

- Do you involve children in decisions about rules, boundaries and consequences?

- Do you take the opportunity, when children question authority, to engage them in debate and encourage them to think autonomously?

---

# Communication and language

Following the rule of law involves being able to pay attention, listen and understand what is expected.

---

## Communication and language

| Aspect | Development statement/ Early Learning Goal | How does this link to the rule of law? | Practice that promotes the rule of law |
|---|---|---|---|
| **Listening and attention** | Gives attention to what others say and responds appropriately. | Following the rule of law requires good listening and attention skills. | Playing games that involve listening to and following verbal instructions. |
| **Understanding** | Follows instructions involving several ideas or actions. | Following the rule of law requires understanding what is expected. | Playing games that involve acting out instructions and following rules. |
| **Understanding** | Answers 'how' and 'why' questions about their experiences and in response to stories or events. | Following the rule of law requires understanding the underlying reasons for rules and restrictions and foreseeing the possible consequences of disregarding them. | Engaging children in discussion about their behaviour and encouraging them to think about the consequences. |
| **Speaking** | Express themselves effectively. | Laws are often broken by people who feel angry, unhappy, misunderstood, resentful and hard done by. | Encouraging children to clearly communicate how they feel verbally instead of hitting out when angry or frustrated. Setting up 'friendship stops' that children can go to when they are having trouble resolving an issue and need an adult to mediate. |

In addition, it requires clear communication to avoid misunderstandings and disagreements that might result in angry feeling and negative behaviour. It is crucial that children understands and appreciate that living under the rule of law protects individual citizens and is essential for their wellbeing and safety.

## Case study: Talking it through

Karolina, Natalia and Emma (age 3/4 years) attend a large nursery where children are encouraged to talk through disagreements and reflect upon their behaviour at 'friendship stops'. There is one friendship stop indoors and another outside.

The girls are playing mermaids. Natalia and Emma decide to swim out to Pirate Island to find some diamond tiaras in a treasure chest (a group of boys are playing pirates nearby). Karolina says she is happy where she is – she already has a tiara. Natalia and Emma shout at Karolina – it is alright for her because she already has a tiara. Emma tries to take Karolina's tiara off her head. Karolina grabs Emma's arm. Emma starts to cry and runs to the friendship stop.

The nursery teacher approaches Emma at the friendship stop and asks her what has happened. After listening to Emma's version of events she asks Karolina to come to the stop and tell her side. Once both girls have calmed down the teacher asks why they think they ended up arguing. Emma responds by suggesting Karolina will not share her tiara.

The teacher asks if they have any ideas what they could have done instead of fighting over the tiara. Emma explains she and Natalia were planning to get more tiaras but Karolina would not help them. The teacher asks Karolina if she thinks it is fair or reasonable to stop the others having their own tiaras. Karolina says not. The teacher asks Emma if she feels snatching the tiara was the right thing to do. Emma shakes her head. The teacher then asks Karolina how she feels about hurting Emma. Karolina looks down and does not answer. The teacher asks what the girls could have done instead and what they can do now to make things better. Emma suggests Karolina could have shared her tiara or helped her get another one. The teacher agrees and encourages the girls to say sorry to each other. They decide to swim to Pirate Island with Natalia in search of more tiaras.

In this example, the teacher encourages the girls to reflect on their behaviour and think about why a small disagreement escalated into an argument where someone got hurt.

## Listening, attending and responding

Listening and attending are essential for all aspects of learning and development. Children who can listen to and follow instructions will be more likely to succeed both in terms of learning and meeting behavioural expectations. Practise listening skills with young children by playing games that require them to attend and respond. Find plenty of ideas for such games in the titles listed in the resources section at the back of this book.

### Simon Whispers

This game is a cross between Simon Says and Chinese Whispers. It requires the children to listen carefully, relay and follow instructions. Ask the children to join into pairs and move into a space. Then walk around the room and whisper an instruction into the ear of one child in each pair. That child should then say the instruction out loud to their partner, who has to do the action. Repeat the game but this time whisper in the ear of the other child in each pair.

Make the game easier for yourself by whispering the same instruction to each pair so you can remember what you've asked everyone to do. Tell the children they should all stand still until you say 'go' so everyone says the instruction out loud at the same time. Explain if you do not whisper 'Simon says' before the instruction they should just stand quiet and still.

## Communicating with each other

Illustrate to children the benefits of talking and listening to each other. Look for opportunities to help them understand

---

### Think about...
...how you help children follow the rule of law by fostering communication skills:

- How often do you take time out to specifically practise listening and attention skills?

- Do you encourage children to talk through their disagreements?

- Do you encourage children to reflect upon their own and others' behaviour?

- How do you help them understand the relationship between their behaviour and the resulting consequences?

- Do you give children strategies for communicating their wants, likes and dislikes rather than lashing out?

the importance of communicating with each other instead of letting events take over, resulting in misunderstandings, disagreements and hurt feelings.

## No thank-you

As well as teaching speaking and listening skills it is helpful to give children strategies for verbally communicating how they feel about unwanted attention or physical contact from others.

For example, encourage them to hold up one hand with palm facing out and say 'Stop' or 'Please don't do that, I don't like it', rather than lashing out or pushing others away.

If you have children with special educational needs (SEN) in the setting, teach them and the other children in the group signs for 'No', 'Stop', 'Sad' and 'Hurt'.

# Literacy

Use characters and events in picture books to explore feelings, behaviour and the concepts of right and wrong, and to help young children make connections between how they feel, how they behave and how this impacts upon themselves and everyone around them.

## Facing up to the consequences

*The Scarecrows' Wedding* by Julia Donaldson and Axel Scheffler (Scholastic) – this story includes a character whose behaviour puts another's life at risk, which is useful for starting a discussion about how an individual's actions can have a negative impact on those around them.

**Reflecting on the story: What might happen if...?** Ask

# Literacy

| Aspect | Development statement/ Early Learning Goal | How does this link to the rule of law? |
|---|---|---|
| **Reading** | Begins to be aware of the way stories are structured; suggests how the story might end; listens to stories with increasing attention and recall; describes main story settings, events and principal characters. | Introduce children to characters who are exploring the concept of right and wrong, and struggling to manage their feelings and behaviour.<br><br>Alternatively, use stories to introduce children to good role models.<br><br>Ask children to empathise with characters and think about why they have done the right/wrong thing, how this has affected others, what they could have done otherwise and how they can make it better.<br><br>Ask them to consider the events in a story as they evolve. Can the children predict what might happen next? What will happen if the character chooses to do the wrong thing? What if they choose to do the right thing? |
| **Reading** | Demonstrates understanding when talking with others about what they have read. | Share stories that have moral messages and explore behaviours and consequences. Ask children to explain what happened. What did the characters do? Were they right or wrong? What were the consequences?<br><br>Encourage children to reflect upon the characters and events in stories and consider them in relation to their own experiences. |

the children what they think of Reginald's behaviour. Did he care about what happened to Betty? What about the consequences of smoking for himself? Ask them to consider what might have happened if Harry had not made it back in time to put the fire out.

Encourage the children to make up their own stories about breaking rules and facing consequences. Set up small world and role play scenarios and place question cards that prompt the children to think about what might happen if…? For example:

● Farm: Place a sign on a gate saying, 'Please close the gate' and a question card asking, 'What might happen if someone leaves a gate open?'

● Zoo: Place a sign on an enclosure saying, 'Do not feed the animals' and a question card asking, 'What might happen if someone feeds the animals?'

● Space ship: Place a sign on the control panel saying, 'Do not press this button' and a question card asking, 'What might happen if you press this button?'

● Doctor surgery: Place a sign on a medical cabinet saying, 'Medicines: Keep away from children and pets' and a question card asking, 'What might happen if the doctor leaves medicines lying around?'

Set up a puppet theatre for children to act out their own scenarios and explore what happens when… Spark ideas by leaving question cards next to the theatre asking:

● Why is Crocodile crying?

● Why did Panda throw his toys on the floor?

● What made Lion roar so loud?

● Why is Hippo hiding from everyone?

● Why won't anyone play with Rabbit?

## Exploring the difference between right and wrong

*Oh No, George!* by Chris Haughton (Walker Books) – George's owner goes off to the shops asking, "Will you be good, George?" George is then left alone with all kinds of tempting opportunities to misbehave. This is a really amusing book about a dog's struggle with right and wrong and great for discussing actions and consequences.

**Reflecting on the story: Making the right decision**
After reading the story through once to give the children a

chance to enjoy the comic timing, read it through a second time but pause to answer the question, "What will George do?" Of course, the children will be able to say what he is about to do because they have heard it already. Lead on from this and ask them what George should do instead and why. Ask if any of the children have misbehaving pets at home. What do they get up to? What are the consequences of their behaviour?

## Making the right decision

*Good Little Wolf* by Nadia Shireen (Jonathan Cape) – Rolf, a good little wolf, who likes being kind and helpful meets the Big Bad Wolf, who cannot understand why someone would want to be so nice. The Big Bad Wolf challenges Rolf to behave more wolf-like and Rolf proves it is possible to be a wolf and be good as well. This book helps children to consider the difference between right and wrong and why it is important they make their own decisions about how they behave. There's also a message about living up (or down) to the expectations that others may have of you… and there is a fun little twist at the end.

**Reflecting on the story: Making our own choices** Ask the children to think about how happy Little Wolf is at the beginning of the story. How do they think he would have felt if he had done all the things the Big Bad Wolf was asking him to do?

# Rule of law

Every so often bring the children together with the Moral Monster (use a monster puppet). Explain the Moral Monster is unlike other monsters, he is a friendly monster who always tries to do the right thing. Sometimes though, he is unsure about what is right and what is wrong so he needs the children to help him make the right decision. Use the monster to pose problems such as:

● His friend will not let him play football so he is considering eating the ball to teach him a lesson.

● His mum will not let him eat cookies before tea so he is thinking about taking the cookies and hiding them.

● He has not had a turn with the cars all morning so he is considering throwing them over the fence when no one is looking.

● He wants to dance but no one wants to play his music so he is thinking about pressing stop on the CD player every time someone puts it on.

● His friend Mischief Monster said he is too good to be a monster so he plans to knock down all the brick models and towers the children build to prove he is just as monstrous as any other monster.

Ask the children to tell the monster what they think about the ideas he has for solving his problems. Can they explain why they think they way they do? Do they have any alternative suggestions for the monster?

## The other side of the story

For some light relief after all the hefty moral consideration of right and wrong there are some fantastic picture books available that retell popular stories from the point of view of the villain:

● *The Wolf's Story* by Toby Forward and Izhar Cohen (Walker) retells the story of Little Red Riding Hood from the perspective of the wolf. Another book that takes a similar approach is The True Story of the 3 Little Pigs by Jon Scieszka and Lane Smith (Puffin). Also, Priscilla Lamont has written two Nursery Rhyme Crimes (Frances Lincoln). These books feature Tom, Tom the Piper's Son, told from the perspective of the pig and Little Bo Peep, told from the perspective of the sheep.

## Understanding the World

The EYFS presents opportunities for finding out about how the rule of law is applied and enforced through understanding the world. Children can learn about the role of a police officer through a topic about people who help us tackling crime and keeping safe and may also reflect upon their own experiences of crime.

Such a topic also opens up the opportunity to help children consider punishment, regret and consequences.

## Understanding the world

| Aspect | Development statement/ Early Learning Goal | How does this link to the rule of law? | Practice that promotes the rule of law |
|---|---|---|---|
| **People and communities** | Shows interest in different occupations and ways of life. | The law is enforced by the police. | Helping children to develop respect for the police officers who enforce the law.<br><br>Explaining what happens to people who break the law. |
| **People and communities** | Talks about past and present events in their own lives and in the lives of family members. | Sharing personal experiences of crime encourages empathy and prompts consideration of consequences. | Helping children to empathise with victims of crime.<br><br>Allowing and enabling children to act out their own experiences and play with ideas and themes involving crime and punishment, e.g. when playing 'bad guys'.* |

*There is a link here with expressive arts and design. Children make sense of their experiences by acting them out, often during small world and role play.

# People who help us

Find out about the role of a police officer.

- Turn the role play area into a police station: Provide uniforms, walkie-talkies, notepads and pencils; set up a desk with a phone and computer; set up a holding cell with a bed; stick police signs on cars, trikes and scooters outside.

- Read information books to find out what a police officer does.

- Invite your local community support officer into the setting. Before the visit ask the children to think of some questions they might like to ask.

- Visit a police station, meet some police officers and see a holding cell.

- Set up a crime scene in the setting: Make it look as if someone or something broke in over night. Turn over tables, open and empty drawers, put muddy footprints on the floor and finger prints on cupboards, doors and tables. Surround the area with crime scene tape (see resources) and set up an incident room.

# Crime and punishment

Talk about what happens to people who break the law in Britain. Explain as well as feeling bad about what they have done, criminals have to suffer consequences including paying a fine, doing community service or going to prison. Discuss the reasons behind each of these punishments.

Explore good and evil. Just because we make mistakes or do something wrong, does it mean we are bad people? Is it possible for good people to do bad things? Is it possible to make things better if you have done something bad?

## The language we use

Think carefully about the language you use when speaking to a child who has done something wrong. It is very important the child understands you are criticising their behaviour and not them as a person. This also applies to any conversations you might have with parents.

# Caring and sharing

Find out if any of the children have ever experienced crime. Have they had anything stolen? Have they had anything vandalised? Do they know anyone else who has experienced crime? How did it make them feel?

## Case study: Everybody makes mistakes

While teaching in a reception class in a maintained two-form entry school I set up and photographed a number of scenarios with a puppet from my class called Indian Brave and a puppet from the parallel class called Claude. In one particular picture the puppets were seen to be arguing with Claude pushing Indian Brave over (see page 25). I used the photo to prompt discussion about how we treat our friends and how to resolve disagreements. Later in the week we had an open plan afternoon when the whole year group were free to move between the classrooms. The children from my class went next door, found Claude and shouted at him for being mean to Indian Brave.

This incident prompted further discussion about misbehaviour, punishment, consequences and treatment of people who do something wrong. It created an opportunity to explore with the children whether going after Claude in such a way was right and helpful. Claude was not a bad person. He had made a mistake and was sorry. He and Indian Brave were friends again.

## Think about...

...how you feel about the children playing 'bad guys'. It is inevitable that children will play games involving 'goodies' and 'baddies'. Consider:

- Whether it is a good idea to place an outright ban on such play or whether you can use it as an opportunity to explore important issues.

- Looking for opportunities to explore what happens to bad guys in role play. Often the bad guy is captured and killed by the good guys. Use this type of play to open up discussion with the children about what might happen in real life. Do we just go around killing people that commit crimes?

- Giving children plenty of space to play chasing games so they run less risk of hurting themselves and each other.

- Helping the children to think about inventive ways to apprehend the bad guys. Can they think of any ways that do not involve physically grabbing and pulling?

- Holland (2003) suggests allowing practitioners to make their own decision about whether to opt in or out of the play. This is a good way of demonstrating personal choice to the children and teaching them that it is alright to say 'No thank you' when asked if they would like to join in with a game they feel uncomfortable playing.

## Expressive arts and design

| Aspect | Development statement/ Early Learning Goal | How can you help children understand and explore emotions through expressive arts? |
|---|---|---|
| **Exploring and using media and materials** | Safely uses and explores with a variety of materials, tools and techniques, experimenting with colour, design, texture and form. | Plan activities that encourage children to think about the colours, textures, movements, sounds and music that can be used to represent different feelings and emotions. |
| **Being imaginative** | Develops preferences for forms of expression; captures experiences and responses with a range of media, such as music, dance and paint and other materials or words; represents their own ideas, thoughts and feelings through art, music, dance, role play and stories. | Provide the resources children need to independently create artworks that convey different emotions and represent how they might be feeling. Share stories that feature characters who experience different emotions and set up small world and role play scenarios for children to re-enact and expand these narratives. |

**Note:** Take care when asking children to share crime stories. Be aware of the types of experiences the children in your setting may have had. If you are a student or new to a setting ensure you speak to other members of staff and find out about the children in your group. It is possible there will be children who do not want to think or talk about their experiences of crime.

## Expressive arts and design

We know behaviour is closely linked to emotions and children can learn to regulate their own behaviour and adhere to the rule of law if they have a better understanding of their own and others' feelings. Encourage children to use their senses and explore emotions through expressive arts and design.

## A little inspiration

Set up interactive sensory emotion displays. Choose an emotion of the week and represent it using a variety of different objects and materials. Set up a table next to a wall display board. Stick up pictures, paintings and photos, and place some objects and a digital tablet on the table. Try the ideas in the table on page 33.

## Expressing emotions through different media

Invite the children to think about how they can convey

different emotions in a variety of ways. Ask them to think about what different emotions might look and sound like.

### Painting emotions

Provide the children with different coloured paints, a variety of painting utensils and different sized and coloured pieces of paper. Invite them to choose an emotion and ask them to think about how they can show that feeling using paint. Let the children come up with their own ideas but if they struggle try inspiring them with the following:

- Anger: Throw red, orange and deep purple paint bombs at large strips of paper outside; stand in paint wearing wellies and stamp onto large sheets of paper.

- Sadness: Sprinkle watery pale blue, grey and white paint from small watering cans onto thick card outside; drag combs through splodges of light blue paint.

- Happiness: Flick bright yellow, pink and orange paint at large strips of paper on the floor outside; print bright patterns with bare feet and hands.

- Fear: Print with large sponges and grey paint onto black sugar paper; print fingerprint tracks with on paper with white paint.

- Shyness: Create fingerprint collages using pastel multicoloured paints.

## Ideas for sensory emotion displays

| Anger | Sadness | Happiness | Fear | Shyness |
|---|---|---|---|---|
| Red and orange backing paper and drapes | Blue and grey backing paper and drapes | Yellow and pink backing paper and drapes | Black and grey backing paper and drapes | Pale pastel coloured backing paper and drapes |
| Rough, spiky rocks and crystals, scouring pads, a bowl of rough gravel, inflated red balloons | A shallow bowl of water mixed with a couple of drops of blue colouring, pallet of watercolour paints | Bowls of brightly coloured fine sand, multicoloured crayons, strips of bright coloured cellophane | Chunks of grey slate, lumps of coal, charcoals, strips of black sugar paper | Frosted mirrors, masks, strips of light coloured tissue paper, small multicoloured periwinkle shells |
| Pictures of volcanoes, storms clouds gathering, animas bearing teeth | Pictures of empty beaches and parks on grey days, autumn leaves in puddles, weeping willows | Pictures of sunshine, blue skies, green meadows, fields of yellow rapeseed, sunflowers | Pictures of dark cave entrances, black silhouettes of trees at night, black panthers | Pictures of flowers with closed petals, animals peering out from burrows and nests |
| Video footage of volcanoes erupting, silverback gorillas beating their chests, tornadoes ripping through towns | Video footage of rain falling, puddles forming, mist gathering over grey still ocean, bare trees with autumn leaves on the floor | Video footage of dolphins swimming in bright blue sea water, view from an aeroplane on a clear sunny day, birds singing in the trees | Video footage of river rapids, huge thundering waterfalls, whirlpools, approaching sand storms, gathering fog | Video footage of tall grass swaying in the breeze, blossom drifting from trees, rabbits running and hiding in holes |
| Drums, cymbals, guiro | Triangle, chimes, recorder | Tambourine, maracas, castanets, bongos | Xylophone, claves, whistle | Egg shakers, sleigh bells |
| Picture of The Great Wave Off Kanazawa by Hokusai | Picture of Waterlilies by Claude Monet | Picture of A Sunday Afternoon by Georges Seurat | Picture of The Scream by Edvard Munch | Picture of Mona Lisa by Leonardo da Vinci |

### Dancing emotions

Play different types of music and encourage the children to listen and think about how it makes them feel. Try the following:

- Anger: Carl Orff – O Fortuna, Carmina Burana

- Sadness: Mozart – Lacrimosa, Requiem

- Happiness: Vivaldi – Four Seasons, Spring & Summer

- Fear: Bela Bartok – Music for Strings, Percussion and Celesta, III

- Shyness: Tchaikovsky – Swan Lake

Dance amongst the children and ask them what kind of emotion they feel when they listen to this music? How does it make them want to move? How does that movement make them feel?

### Emotive poetry

Help the children compose poems about different emotions. Bring them together in small groups and ask them to think of words to describe various feelings. Ask them to consider how each of those feelings might make them behave. Refer to the books of Brian Moses (see page 24) as examples and offer the following prompts:

*Anger is like…*
*When I am angry I feel like…*
*Anger makes me want to…*
*Anger sounds like…*
*Anger looks like…*
*Anger smells like…*
*If anger was an animal it would be…*

# Individual liberty

People in Britain have a right to personal freedom. This means British citizens should be free to make their own choices, voice personal opinions and portray their individual identity without fear of oppression, discrimination or censure. In order to exercise personal freedom people need self-belief and self-awareness because not only does this give them the self-confidence to express themselves, it also helps to prevent them looking outwards and hurting others; those who persecute others often suffer from low self-esteem themselves.

When considering how to teach children about individual liberty in the early years it is helpful to think about what personal freedom means to young children, how we can help them exert their right to this freedom and how we can encourage them to respect the freedom of others.

**Individual identity:** Children should be encouraged to express their opinions and talk about their likes and dislikes. They should also be asked to reflect on their differences and respect the rights of others to think and choose differently from them.

**Self-confidence:** Practitioners should nurture individuality and help children feel secure and happy about who they are. In addition, children should be taught that mistakes are a part of learning and feel they can take risks without fear of failure and ridicule.

**Freedom of choice:** The early learning environment should support individual interests and aptitudes and allow children to play and explore in their own ways. This means giving children options and allowing them to make their own choices.

**Freedom of expression:** In the early years this involves helping children to develop the communication and language skills they need to express their ideas and opinions, as well as to listen to the views of others. It also involves encouraging them to find their own preferred means of artistic expression.

It is possible to promote individual liberty and help children develop a positive sense of self, as well as respect for the rights and freedoms of others through the following EYFS areas of learning and development.

## Personal, social and emotional development

To celebrate the right to individual liberty children first

need to have a sense of self and positive self-esteem. Furthermore, they should also have the freedom to explore and experiment and find out what makes them tick; what is it that grabs their attention and what truly inspires them to want to learn more? This is promoted in the EYFS under the self-confidence and self-awareness aspect of personal, social and emotional development.

## Individual identity

Every individual is a product of their social, familial and cultural background. Early years practitioners can help children to develop a positive sense of personal identity and pride by encouraging them to talk about themselves and share their experiences.

## Personal, social and emotional development

| Aspect | Development statement/ Early Learning Goal | How does this link to individual liberty? | Practice that promotes individual liberty |
|---|---|---|---|
| **Self-confidence and self-awareness** | Expresses own preferences and interests; confident to talk to other children when playing, and will communicate freely about own home and community. | Self-knowledge and a sense of personal identity is at the heart of individual liberty. | Helping children to develop their self-knowledge and explore their personal identities. Inviting children to talk about their homes, lives and families. Supporting children's rights to think and behave differently from others. Helping children to accept others may have different preferences. |
| **Self-confidence and self-awareness** | Can describe self in positive terms and talk about abilities; confident to try new activities. | Enjoying individual liberty involves having confidence and a positive sense of self. | Celebrating children's individual personalities. Encouraging children to be themselves and letting them know you like and respect them for who they are. Creating a safe learning environment where children are encouraged to take risks and are not afraid of failing. |
| **Self-confidence and self-awareness** | Confident to try new activities, and say why they like some activities more than others; confident to speak in a familiar group, will talk about their ideas, and will choose the resources they need for their chosen activities. | Individual liberty involves having the freedom and opportunity to choose a particular direction and follow personal interests. | Providing a learning environment that represents a variety of interests and aptitudes. Giving children time and space to explore their interests and indulge in self-directed activity of their choice. Regularly observing the children to find out what truly interests them and using these observations to inform planning and provide resources and activities that build on these interests. |

## Who am I?

Send home a large sheet of paper with a big spidergram featuring branches that lead out to the following headings: Home, family, pets, town/village, friends, favourite places, favourite stories, hobbies, favourite toys, special talents/ abilities. Insert a blank box under each heading for the children to stick photos, draw pictures and add captions. Include a blank space in the centre of the page for a photo of the child.

Invite the children to share their spidergrams either with the whole setting or their key worker groups. Ask the children in the group to think about how they are similar and different to each other. Can they pick out anything special or interesting about each other? Perhaps they have a special talent, have an unusual pet or come from an interesting place.

## Who are we?

Help to convey the message that every group is composed of a set of individuals, who collectively make the group all the richer.

● Create a large wall display featuring a fantasy fruit tree.

● Work with the children in small groups and ask them to each draw and cut out a picture of their favourite fruit (they are free to make up a fantasy fruit if they choose). Ask them to explain why they have chosen or created that particular fruit. Stick photos of their faces on their fruits.

● Give each child three pre-cut large green leaf shapes. Ask them to think of three words that describe themselves. They can then write the words on the leaves or you can scribe for them.

● Stick the fruits surrounded by the associated leaves on the display tree.

● Bring the children together and read out some of the words they have used to describe themselves. Point out the range of descriptions and how many different personalities there are in the group.

● To extend the activity get the children to think of words to describe each other. Record these on lighter coloured leaves and add them to the tree.

## Self-confidence

Individual liberty gives people the right to express themselves and voice their views and opinions. If someone has a positive sense of self they will be more confident and at ease with themselves, enabling them to celebrate and enjoy their individuality and making them more willing to stand in the spotlight and be scrutinised by others. Plan activities that help children to identify their strengths and grow in self-confidence.

## I am super!

One way of getting children to describe themselves in positive terms is to get them to create superheroes with special powers that represent their own unique abilities and talents. Bring the children together in small groups and ask them to think about what they are good at. If they were superheroes how would these talents translate into super powers? For example, someone who is good at running might be able to run at hyper speed as a superhero; someone who is good at singing might be able to reduce buildings to rubble using only their voice; and someone who is kind and caring may have the ability to build walls around others to protect them. See where the children's imaginations take them.

## Freedom of choice

Early years practitioners have the freedom to plan a curriculum based around the children's interests. They observe children to identify their needs, aptitudes, abilities and fascinations, and use these observations to inform and develop future planning that is relevant and inspiring. This child-centred pedagogy promotes individual liberty because it puts children at the centre of their own education; they choose what they want to learn about and how.

### Case study: Planning projects that build on the interests of the children

A group of nursery children from Horton Grange Primary School in Bradford went to visit a local farm. During the visit a farmer brought out a chicken and, to the children's surprise, produced an egg from under the chicken as if by magic. On return to the setting this was the event that stood out from the day and dominated the children's conversation.

The teacher decided to build on this interest and plan a project all about eggs (Sargent, 2011). She asked the children what they already knew about eggs and what they wanted to find out. Over the following three weeks the children learned about where eggs come from, how they get to the supermarket and how they can be prepared and eaten. They experimented with breaking eggs, examined the properties of raw and cooked egg and played with egg shell. The project culminated in the hire of an incubator from a local farm and the hatching of some chicks.

This is an example of promoting individual liberty by building on the interests of the children and following their chosen direction.

## Knowing your own mind

Children with positive self-esteem are also more likely to feel secure in the choices they make. There is an important link with rule of law here. The Prevent strategy suggests 'group bonding, peer pressure and indoctrination' lead to the acceptance of an extremist rhetoric that validates the use of violence in support of a cause (HM Government, 2011, p.17). It might be argued, therefore, that we need to help children develop a sense of the difference between right and wrong and give them the strength to make a stand if they feel something is not right. Such self-assurance will empower children to make their own decisions instead of bowing down to pressure to follow the crowd.

# Communication and language

Individual liberty includes the right to freedom of expression. The EYFS aims to equip children with the listening, attention, understanding and speaking skills they need to exercise this right and support the right of others through the communication and language area of learning and development.

## Respecting others' right to be heard

Freedom of speech is a two-way street. There is no point in having the freedom to express views and opinions if no one is listening. What's more, it is important to be able to listen to others because no one lives in a vacuum and opinions affect how people feel and think. If people do not listen to how others respond they will be unable to appreciate and understand the possible impact that their words may have.

## Respecting difference in opinion

In the same way that freedom of speech relies upon the ability of people to listen, it also depends on the acceptance that people have of differing views and opinions. Encourage children to talk and listen to each other by presenting them with collaborative challenges that require them to work together but can be approached in more than one way. For example:

- Make a fire engine for the role play area out of a large cardboard box and junk.

- Go on a treasure hunt or set up a treasure hunt for another group.

- Build the tallest tower you can using wooden blocks.

- Arrange pictures from a story in the correct order then retell the story.

- Navigate an obstacle course and get a teddy from one end to the other without touching the floor.

- Make a diorama for a small world play scene.

- Make a kite that flies.

- Rescue a teddy bear that is stuck in a tree.

Split the children into small groups and allocate an adult to each. Begin by asking each group to share their ideas about how they are going to tackle the challenge. The adults should encourage the children to listen to each others' ideas and help them consider the merits of each by asking questions. Once the children have decided how they are going to approach the challenge, the adults should stay with them and help them to share out the tasks, and gather the equipment they need, while continuing to listen to each other and work together. Vicki Charlesworth (2009) provides a detailed explanation of this approach with many examples, demonstrating how this can be accomplished with very young children.

## Case study: Helping children understand the benefits of listening

It is Alicia's (age 4) turn to show and tell. She has brought in a wormery in a jar and is explaining to a class of 29 reception children how she made it. Three children at the back are whispering amongst themselves. The teacher asks them what they are whispering about. One of the children responds by asking how the worms have managed to stay alive inside a jar. The teacher turns to Alicia and asks if she can explain. Alicia points out the holes her father has punched in the top of the jar so the worms can breath and says she puts grated vegetable peelings on the top of the soil every couple of days for them to eat.

The teacher praises the child for his question, then says next time instead of whispering to his friends he should put his hand up. That way he and the others around him will be able to continue to listen without missing anything. He will also get the chance to have his question answered and everyone else will benefit from learning the answer at the same time.

In this example, the teacher resists the temptation to chastise the children at the back for whispering and instead invites them to share. She then uses the interruption to exemplify how taking turns at speaking and listening benefits everyone as a whole.

# Individual liberty

## Communication and language

| Aspect | Development statement/ Early Learning Goal | How does this link to individual liberty? | Practice that promotes individual liberty |
|---|---|---|---|
| **Listening and attention** | Gives attention to what others say and responds appropriately. | Individual liberty means respecting others' right to express their views and opinions.* | Modelling good listening skills.<br><br>Playing games that practise listening skills; encouraging children to listen attentively in order to offer an appropriate response (see page 27).<br><br>Asking children questions that require a considered response.<br><br>Helping children to accept that others may think differently to them.<br><br>Helping children to understand there might be more than one way to approach something. |
| **Understanding** | Answers 'how' and 'why' questions about their experiences and in response to stories or events. | Having a good understanding of issues is important when exercising the right to free speech. | Fostering sustained shared thinking; encouraging children to talk about their ideas, make links, question how things work, think about how to solve problems, and ask why things happen.<br><br>Encouraging children to ask questions. |
| **Speaking** | Express themselves effectively, showing awareness of listeners' needs. | Individual liberty means having the right to free speech. | Ensuring children are allowed to express their views and opinions.<br><br>Introducing children to a wide range of vocabulary so they are able to express their thoughts, views, ideas and opinions more clearly.<br><br>Giving children the opportunity to practise speaking clearly and confidently.<br><br>Ensuring children who speak English as an additional language (EAL) and with special educational needs (SEN) are given the tools to enable them to communicate. |

*There is a link here to democracy. In a democratic society everyone should have a right to participate and contribute, which includes exercising the right to voice views and opinions.

## Gaining a more in-depth understanding

Free speech is more effective if the speaker knows what they are talking about. It was the contention of early education theorists Lev Vygotsky and Jerome Bruner that high quality adult-child interactions are vital for helping children develop good knowledge and understanding and move on in their learning. This is supported by the findings of the contemporary longitudinal research study Effective Provision of Pre-School Education (EPPE). Here researchers describe such interactions as 'sustained shared thinking', where two or more people share thoughts and compare ideas in order to clarify their thinking and make better sense of the problem or concept they are considering (Siraj-Blatchford and Sylva et al, 2004, p.vi).

Take as many opportunities as possible throughout each day to involve children in conversation and debate that gets them thinking and questioning, helping to improve their knowledge and understanding of different issues and concepts. Try the following:

### Display open questions around the learning environment

Print out open questions in a large font, mount them on bright coloured card and laminate them. Stick them on walls and cupboards all around the setting. These will serve as prompts for practitioners, who can catch them at a

glance and use them during conversations with children to get them thinking.

### Create sustained shared thinking cards

Create sustained shared thinking cards to display in each area of provision around the setting. On each card list key vocabulary and question ideas that can be introduced into conversation. Find a set of these cards amongst the printable resources in *The Project Approach in Early Years Provision* (Sargent, 2011).

### Interactive and informative displays

Set up low level displays linked to your current topic or theme with objects, artefacts, photos, posters and children's comments and questions. Bring children to the displays to examine the objects and pictures and consider the questions and comments of others.

## Freedom of expression

In order to enjoy the right to free speech a person needs to be able to express themselves clearly. It is therefore important to set up a learning environment that encourages children to practise their speaking skills. Try the following:

- Listen out for their interests and set out small world and role play resources they will be enthusiastic about.

- Hide strange objects in the shrubbery in the outdoor area for the children to discover and wonder about.

- Source posters featuring illustrated poems, display them at child-eye level around the setting and read them out to children as they pass by.

- Set up a stage and provide costumes, props and microphones.

- Set up a puppet theatre.

- Plan regular singing and rhyme time.

- Use puppets to host question and answer sessions at the end of story times.

### What about the quiet ones?

There will always be children in the group who lack in confidence and prefer not to speak aloud. It is easy for these children to slip through the net, while other louder voices dominate group and carpet times. The following strategies are useful for ensuring everyone gets an equal chance to contribute. Of course, each strategy must be used with the personalities and abilities of individual children in mind; some children may not be ready to speak out loud in front of everyone:

- No hands up: Explain you are going to ask a question and could choose anyone to answer so there is no need to put hands up. This strategy encourages everyone to listen in case they are picked. It also gives the practitioner the opportunity to give quiet children a chance to answer.

- Out of a hat: Explain you are going to draw names out of a hat and whoever is picked is the speaker. This random selection method is useful when questioning but also when picking children to come out to the front and speak. It takes the onus off the practitioner to choose and ensures equality of opportunity.

- Talk partners: Explain you would like everyone to discuss the question with a partner. Give the children a few minutes to talk and observe carefully to ensure everyone has a chance to speak. Then ask each pair to feed back. This is a good way of encouraging less confident children to speak because they only have to talk to one person instead of the whole group. When it is time to feed back to everyone else the more confident child can do the talking.

## Giving children a voice

As well as encouraging children to speak and share their ideas within the setting, think about how you can get their voices heard in the outside world. Children are part of the local community and have a right to participate. With a little help children can share their views and opinions. Try the following:

- Set up a social media account for your setting and ask the children what they would like to share.
  - Remember to get parents' written consent before posting comments from or photos of children on social media.
  - Social media accounts should be assigned an administrator who is responsible for monitoring them regularly to remove any dubious or potentially

offensive posts. Ensure privacy settings are set to private to ensure only 'friends' and 'followers' are able to view information.

- Involve the children in local campaigns, for instance road safety, litter/dog fouling issues, saving green spaces or redesigning the local play park.
  - Invite the children to tell you their views on the issue.
  - Help them to create publicity posters that put across their views.
  - Approach relevant organisations and ask them to consider using the children's work to support their campaigns.
  - Help the children write a letter to local government representatives or newspapers.

- Ask children to choose a charity and help them fundraise to support it.
  - Introduce the children to some charities and ask them to vote on which to support.
  - Ask them for fundraising ideas. Again, vote to choose one.
  - Get the children to help publicise the event, for example by making fliers.
  - On the day of the event invite the local media to come along to speak to the children about what they are doing.

- Ask the local library if they might allocate some display

### Case study: Getting young children's voices heard

At the time of going to press Parklands Nursery School in Northampton was participating in the BRIC Project, a research study exploring the democratic involvement of young children in public and civic spaces (BRIC, 2016). As part of the project nursery staff explored ways they could get children's voices out in the local community including forging links with a well-known local bookstore. The children wrote reviews about books they had purchased in the store and these were displayed in the children's section.

- Giving the children physical signs they can use to communicate with, for example, thumbs up/down.

- If you have children in the class who use Makaton, Signalong, or British Sign Language (BSL) teach the other children some key signs so they can communicate with those children more easily.

# Literacy

Use characters and events in picture books to help children explore personal identity and to understand what individual liberty means. In addition, invite children to exercise their right to freedom of expression by reviewing books and giving their personal opinions about which stories they most or least enjoy and why.

## Individual identity

*Charlie and Lola: My Completely Best Story Collection* by Lauren Child (Puffin) – Lola is a fabulously quirky individual with a bright and sparky personality, making her ideal for exploring individuality. Young children easily identify with Lola's voice and relate to the issues she struggles with.

**Reflecting on these stories: Lola's way** Once the children are familiar with a range of Charlie and Lola stories

space for local children to showcase their favourite books and stories with drawings and reviews.

## Ensuring all children are able to communicate

Everyone should have the right to individual liberty and freedom of speech and it is important to consider how children learning EAL, with SEN or speech and language delay can also enjoy these rights. This means thinking about how you can ensure they are able to understand and follow activities and discussions, as well as actively participate and communicate their own thoughts and ideas. Consider the following:

- Using visual prompts and physical gestures to make it easier for these children to follow what you are saying.

- Making key word fans with pictures for the children to use when they are trying to tell you something.

- Pairing children up into talk partners during question and answer sessions.

- Utilising support assistants carefully to assist children who need help communicating in a variety of situations.

---

**Think about...**

...how you help children to exercise their right to free speech as well as encourage them to listen to others:

- Do you specifically plan activities that practise speaking and listening skills?

- How do you foster a thinking environment where children are encouraged to consider how things work and why things happen?

- How do you ensure group and carpet times are not dominated by the same voices and everyone has a chance to speak?

- How do you ensure everyone's opinions are taken into account?

- How do you enable children learning EAL or with SEN are able to fully participate and voice their views and opinions?

---

## Literacy

| Aspect | Development statement/ Early Learning Goal | How can you use stories to explore the concept of personal freedom and promote individual liberty? |
|---|---|---|
| **Reading** | Listens to stories with increasing attention and recall; describes main story settings, events and principal characters. | Introduce children to characters who have strong personal identities. Celebrate characters that are different.\n\nEncourage the children to think about what they like about different characters. What is it that makes a character stand out?\n\nShare stories that ponder issues related to individual liberty and use them to encourage children to think about personal freedoms. |
| **Reading** | Enjoys an increasing range of books; demonstrates understanding when talking with others about what they have read. | Invite children to share their thoughts and opinions about stories and books. Ask them:<br>• What do they like/dislike about the characters?<br>• What do they like/dislike about the story?<br>• What do they think about the ending?<br>• Would they change the story? If so, how?<br>• What do they think of the illustrations? |

ask them what they like about Lola. What is it about her character that makes her different? Reflect upon how Lola handles different situations and ask the children to think about why she might do the things she does (many of the stories in this series can also be used to explore behaviour and consequences). Ask the children if they can think of any characters they like from other books. Why do they like these characters so much?

Provide collage and junk modelling materials for the children to create robots that reflect their own individual personalities. Explain they can either create a collaged picture or build a model. The children are free to create anything they choose – anything goes. Give them some examples of how they might represent themselves through the activity. For instance:

• Bright colours for an outgoing robot.

• Lots of buttons for a robot that likes computers and gadgets.

• Shutters for the eyes for a shy robot.

• Big hands and feet for a robot that likes physical games and sports.

• A big mouth for a robot that likes singing, shouting and talking.

• Patterns for a robot that likes arts and crafts.

• Themed robots that reflect interests such as pirates, fairies, dinosaurs or clowns.

When the robots are completed invite the children to show their creations and explain the thinking behind their designs. What does their robot say about them?

## Self-confidence

*What I Like About Me* by Allia Zobel-Nolan (Reader's Digest Children's Books) – this book features a host of children who are all different for one reason or another. Each of the children celebrate their differences and a mirror on the last page invites the reader to celebrate theirs also. This book aims to boost self-confidence by helping children understand being an individual is a good thing.

**Reflecting on the book: What I like about me** Sit in a

circle to share this book. At the end pass it around for each child to look in the mirror and tell everyone something they like about themselves. Then pass the book around again but this time ask the child with the book to hold the mirror up to the child next to them and say something they like about their peer.

Make personalised t-shirts. Provide fabric crayons and iron-on motifs for the children to design t-shirts that reflect their individual personalities and strengths. Challenge the children to think of a slogan that represents who they are and help them write it on the back.

## Different perspectives

*Two Monsters* by David McKee (Andersen Press) – the monsters in this story are not willing to try and see things from each other's point of view and instead hurl insults and rocks, eventually tearing down a mountain in temper. It is a great story for illustrating the importance of listening to others and considering how quickly a situation can get out of hand when people are dismissive of each other's point of view and anger begins to build.

**Reflecting on the story: Listening to one another**
Encourage the children to think about what might have happened in this story if the monsters had listened to each other in the first place. The monsters actually agree with each other; they just see things from different perspectives. Ask the children to consider what might have happened if the monsters had completely disagreed about something – how much worse it could have been. What can we do when we disagree with someone else? Should we dismiss others' thoughts and ideas just because we do not agree?

## Freedom of choice

*Zog* by Julia Donaldson and Axel Scheffler (Alison Green Books) – in this story Zog the dragon is treated for a series of ailments by a girl he later discovers to be a princess. When Sir Gadabout the knight arrives to rescue the princess she dismisses a life of prancing around in frilly dresses and declares she wants to be a doctor. This story delivers the message that it does not matter who you are or where you come from, you should have the right to do anything you choose.

**Reflecting on the story: Personal aspirations** Use the story to get the children thinking about what they want to do when they get older. Invite them to talk about their interests and think about the types of careers they might enjoy. Challenge any stereotypical thinking that may surface, for example, the idea that some jobs are for boys and others for girls.

## Our favourite books

Invite children to exercise their right to express an opinion by reviewing story books. Write to parents asking for a photo of them reading a favourite book with their child. Send home a book review template for them to fill in together. This could include the following questions:

- Book title:

- Author and illustrator:

- What do you like about this book?

- Is there anything you would change?

- How often do you read this book?

Create a display featuring the photos and book reviews. If the children do not mind bringing their books in, display these also on a table nearby with a pile of blank book review slips for the children to fill in if they wish.

Extend the activity by sending home different books for the children to read and review. Share the book reviews with the rest of the group and see who agrees or disagrees with the various opinions.

## Expressive arts and design

| Aspect | Development statement/ Early Learning Goal | How does this link to individual liberty? | Practice that promotes individual liberty |
|---|---|---|---|
| **Exploring and using media and materials** | Understands that different media can be combined to create new effects; manipulates materials to achieve a planned effect; safely uses and explores a variety of materials, tools and techniques, experimenting with colour, design, texture form and function. | Individual liberty means having the right to freedom of expression in any chosen way. | Providing the resources and materials children need to be able to express themselves in a variety of ways.<br><br>Carefully observing and using observations to provide enhancements that will extend children's creative projects and thought processes. |
| **Being imaginative** | Develops preferences for forms of expression; represents their own ideas, thoughts and feelings through design and technology, art, music, dance, role play and stories. | Individual liberty means having the right to freedom of expression in any chosen way. | Exposing children to a wide range of art and creative expression, and talking about meaning and how different artworks make them feel.<br><br>Inviting children to offer their views and opinions about different artworks.<br><br>Giving children time and space to become immersed in their own creative projects.<br><br>Asking children to talk about their art and explain their thinking behind what they have created. |

# Expressive arts and design

As well as expressing themselves verbally, children should be enabled and encouraged to explore and express their individuality through the creative arts and design.

## Freedom of expression

Children express themselves in all kinds of ways. They may stand up and speak out, make up songs an poems and perform them, write stories, play out ideas through small world and role play, draw cartoons, paint pictures and create sculptures. These are all ways they communicate messages and express thoughts, feelings and ideas to others.

### Fostering creativity
Facilitate this creative expression by ensuring children have access to a range of resources and materials along with time and space to use them. Set these resources out in ways that encourage children think differently and consider using things in a way they might not have done before. For example:

- Allow children to select from and help themselves to different types of art resource:
  - O Arrange bottles of poster paint, tubs of powder paint and trays of watercolours in such a way that children can pour and spoon them out by themselves. This may encourage them to mix colours and combine types of paint.
  - O Place trays of crayons, chalks, charcoals and pens amongst paints and craft materials, again to encourage children to mix media.
  - O Provide glue sticks, PVA glue, scissors, sellotape, staplers, card, lolly sticks and pipe cleaners alongside drawing and painting materials to encourage children to add extra dimensions to their art works.

- Combine art materials with natural objects.
  - O Provide tubs of stones, sand, leaves, seeds, pinecones,

# Case study: Individual creative expression

Reflections Nursery & Forest School in Worthing draws its inspiration from the pre-schools of Reggio Emilia in northern Italy and the forest kindergartens of Denmark. It has four ateliers (art studios) and employs four atelieristas (artists) and the children regularly engage in long-term project work, usually inspired and led by their own ideas and interests.

Practitioners set up spaces and offer materials and ideas to the children, and spend a lot of time observing and reflecting upon what they see as the children communicate their thoughts and ideas through different modes of expression. In recent years Reflections has published a number of books documenting the children's explorations. One such book, *The Revolutionary Baby* (Magnavacchi and Wilenski, 2015), documents the thoughts and creations of the children during a year-long focus on 'storying', otherwise described as the narrative languages arising from children's everyday play and independent investigations.

The story of the revolutionary baby emerged from a two-year-old girl who was inspired by other children, who were exploring and creating narratives around danger and safety involving volcanoes, dinosaurs and storms as well as family, home and rescue. She built two different physical worlds out of clay, introduced some clay blob babies and created a story about a 'baby place' and a 'monster place'. She singled out one of the larger blobs, describing it as a 'big strong baby', who could look after the other babies.

An atelierista relayed this story to the wider group and offered them papier mâché, inspiring the children to make a larger version of the two places. The children then worked together using the papier mâché and incorporating art materials, junk and natural objects to create a 'baby place' under a table in the atelier and a 'monster place' on top. What emerged were two contrasting worlds, a safe comfortable space for babies and a dark dangerous space for monsters.

In the little girl's original clay creation, she had built a wall to separate the babies and protect them from the monsters and was insistent that the two places remain separate. This idea was picked up on and expanded by the other children and reflected in the larger creation, where babies were not allowed in the monster place and vice versa.

Then a practitioner introduced a tiny inch-long model of a baby to the scene. The children viewed this baby differently to the others. It was not vulnerable like the other babies; it was a big, strong fighting hero allowed to break the rules and travel between the baby and monster worlds. The tiny baby triggered exploration of a number of themes including good and bad, power and vulnerability, and danger and defiance.

This is a wonderful example of how early years practitioners can provide an environment that invites children to use their own individual creativity to express their ideas, thoughts and feelings. The children had access to time, space, resources and each other's ideas to create a story setting and narrative that explored a range of oppositional themes as they tried to make sense of the world in their own way. There is also a link to democracy here. The girl who provoked this story is actually very quiet. However, the practitioners in this setting spend a great deal of time observing and listening to the children. This means all children, including the quiet ones, are encouraged to express themselves and enabled to share their ideas. In this case, a story created by a quiet child had a profound creative influence over the other children around her.

twigs, pebbles and shells for children to incorporate into their paintings, drawings, clay and junk models.
- Cut fruit and vegetables in half and leave them next to paints for printing.

- Display pieces of artwork and play music from a range of genres in the art area to inspire the children as they create.

- Read out a poem at the beginning of each week and have an informal chat about it, asking the children what they think it means and how it makes them feel.
  - Choose favourite poems, write them out on large pieces of paper and leave them for the children to decorate. Then cover them in sticky-backed plastic and display them.

- Invite children to bring poems in from home and share them with the rest of the group.
- Play with words and rhymes. Make up silly poems on the spot and ask the children to think of rhyming words, whether they make sense or not. Read some Michael Rosen for inspiration (see resources).

- As well as reading stories make time for an oral storytelling each day. Tell traditional tales and fables and discuss their morals and messages.
  - Set up puppet theatres for the children to retell, enhance and extend these stories.
  - Place book versions of the stories on a staged area with costumes and props and encourage the children to make up their own characters and alter the plots.

O Provide a selection of musical instruments for the children to use to enhance their performance or add songs to the storytelling.

● Inspire children to sing and dance.
  O Set up a stage for the children to give performances to each other.
  O Provide a CD or MP3 player for them to select and play music.
  O Provide costumes as well as fabrics for them to create their own outfits.
  O Give the children instruments to make their own music.

## Viewing personal opinions

Invite children to voice their own critical opinions about artworks.

● Take them to galleries and museums and expose them to a wide range of art in various forms. Ask them what they think about the different creations. What do they like and why?

● Play different genres of music throughout the day in the setting. Ask the children for their opinions about the different types of music. What is their favourite music and why? What type of music do they dislike?

● Take the children to your local theatre or invite a theatre company in to the setting. After the performance ask the children what they thought. Did they enjoy it? Why/why not? What was their favourite part/character?

### Think about...
...how you actively promote creativity and freedom of expression in your setting.

● How do you encourage children to express themselves in a variety of different ways?

● Are art resources easily accessible to the children?

● Do you encourage children to combine different media or is everything neatly stored in its place?

● Do you plan narrow craft activities with pre-prepared materials or do you start with an idea and let the children interpret it in their own way?

● Do you make time to inspire children with stories and poetry?

● How do you encourage children to tell stories of their own?

# Mutual respect and tolerance of different faiths and beliefs

Britain is a diverse society where people of different races, faiths, beliefs and cultural backgrounds should expect to live and work together peacefully. To ensure a respectful and tolerant society of the future children must learn not only to accept and respect difference, but appreciate the value of diversity and the rich opportunities it presents. Therefore, when thinking about how to promote mutual respect and tolerance in the early years it is helpful to consider the following underlying principles:

**Inclusion:** Practitioners should create an inclusive learning environment where all children and their families feel welcome and comfortable, and negative and discriminatory attitudes are challenged. The learning environment should reflect this positive attitude in its communications, displays and resources.

**Tolerance, respect and understanding:** Young children should be introduced to a variety of cultures and traditions,

helping them to understand and respect different faiths and beliefs. They should also learn that human society is comprised of many people of various races, faiths, beliefs, cultures, genders, ages, sexualities and with disabilities. Discriminatory attitudes and behaviour often stem from ignorance and fear. Children should be encouraged to explore similarities and differences between themselves and others so they grow up understanding and appreciating difference.

**Appreciation and celebration:** Early years practitioners should encourage children to value and celebrate diversity. Individual children should be made to feel proud of their cultural heritage and familial background. Settings should do everything possible to make all children and families feel valued and appreciated for what they bring.

It is possible to promote mutual respect and tolerance

of different faiths and beliefs and encourage children to appreciate and celebrate diversity through the following EYFS areas of learning and development.

# Personal, social and emotional development

It is crucial to promote mutual respect and tolerance of different faiths and beliefs and to challenge negative and discriminatory attitudes from the earliest age to ensure children grow up to support these values and form a tolerant and cohesive future society. The EYFS supports this endeavour through personal, social and emotional development.

# An inclusive and cohesive learning community

A fully inclusive setting will acknowledge, respect, include and provide for children and families of all faiths, beliefs and cultures. It will also promote respect for people of different genders, ages, sexualities and with disabilities. This will be reflected in an inclusive ethos and cohesive learning community. For example:

- Displays will reflect the diversity of British society and include people of different races, faiths, beliefs, cultures, genders, ages, sexualities and with disabilities.

- Books and stories will feature characters from a range of

## Personal, social and emotional development

| Aspect | Development statement/ Early Learning Goal | How does this link to mutual respect and tolerance? | Practice that promotes mutual respect and tolerance of different faiths and beliefs |
|---|---|---|---|
| **Making relationships** | Shows sensitivity to others' needs and feelings, and forms positive relationships with adults and other children. | Individual liberty means having the right to freedom of expression in any chosen way. | Fostering a respectful, inclusive and cohesive learning community.\n\nEncouraging children to be kind to each other and think about how others may feel.\n\nMaking arrangements to ensure children and families who speak EAL are included and have access to the same information as everyone else. |
| **Self-confidence and self-awareness** | Confident to talk to other children when playing, and will communicate freely about own home and community; can describe self in positive terms and talk about abilities. | Mutual respect and tolerance means making people feel proud of their racial and cultural background, religious beliefs and family. | Demonstrating an interest in children's cultural background and religious beliefs.\n\nEncouraging children to feel proud of their cultural heritage, religious beliefs and family.\n\nEncouraging children learning EAL to continue using their first language. |
| **Managing feelings and behaviour** | Talks about their own and others' behaviour, and its consequences, and knows that some behaviour is unacceptable. | Mutual respect and tolerance means challenging negative attitudes and discriminatory behaviour and remarks. | Challenging negative and discriminatory attitudes and remarks, whether these are intentional or inadvertently offensive.\n\nEncouraging children to consider their thoughts and actions and how they might affect others. |

## Case study: Challenging misguided and potentially offensive comments

Kofi (age 5) is working in a group with four other children. As part of a whole school 'Magic and Monsters' event the reception children have been split into groups and asked to make up a story about a monster. Each group is working with an adult who is writing down the children's ideas and helping them to structure their story. Later the children will be invited to act out their stories in front of the class.

Kofi's group makes up a story about a volcano rock monster that has stolen a golden key from some pirates. The key is for a treasure chest on a nearby island. A group of brave children must enter the volcano, get the key and find the treasure before the pirates catch them. When it comes to discussing which roles the children are going to play, Adam (age 4) turns to Kofi and says, 'You should be the rock monster because you are brown like rocks'.

Adam does not appear to mean any offence with his suggestion, however, Kofi gets angry and starts to cry. He shouts that he does not want to be the rock monster, he wants to be a brave explorer. The support assistant consoles Kofi and explains he can play whichever role he wants to. She asks Kofi if he would like to explain to Adam how the comment made him feel, but he shakes his head.

She challenges this inadvertently offensive comment by gently explaining to Adam why it is inappropriate. She tells him she understands he did not mean to offend Kofi but choosing someone to be something on account of their skin colour could upset them. Everybody's skin is different and no one should be singled out because of their skin colour.

## Case study: Innocent comments as conversation starters

Edie (age 3) is on a trip to the park with her nursery, which is situated in a predominantly white neighbourhood. While the children are eating a picnic lunch Edie points to a passer-by and says, 'That lady has brown skin'. The teacher nods and says she does. She invites all the children to look at the skin on their arms and compare them with each other. This starts a discussion about skin colour and skin tone. The teacher explains everyone's skin is a different colour and some have darker skin than others. Later, on returning to the setting she brings out a copy of *Ten Little Fingers and Ten Little Toes* by Mem Fox and Helen Oxenbury (Walker), a beautifully illustrated book that delivers the message that everyone is different but in many ways also the same.

In this example the teacher takes the comment as an opportunity to start a conversation about difference in skin colour. She keeps the conversation at the children's level by not complicating the issue and talking about race. She simply invites the children to explore their differences and delivers the message that although everyone looks different it is of no consequence and deep down we are all the same.

---

cultures and challenge gender and racial stereotyping. They will also feature different types of family, including adoptive, foster, single and same sex parents.

- Toys and resources will reflect a range of cultures and faiths.

- Notices and information on the parents' display will be translated into relevant languages.

- Providers will do everything in their power to provide translated letters and important documents for parents who do not speak English, and to acquire the assistance of a translator for meetings.

- The setting will celebrate festivals from different faiths.

- Children will be introduced to art and music from different cultures.

- Stories from around the world will be integrated into literacy planning.

- Signs and labelling will be translated into relevant languages for EAL learners and accompanied by Makaton symbols or Braille lettering for children with SEN and disabilities.

- EAL learners and children with disabilities and SEN will not be separated from the rest of the group.

- Children will be encouraged to support each other, for example through the use of a buddy system or mixed language and ability groups.

- Parents of children with SEN and disabilities will be invited into the setting to advise practitioners about how to organise the learning environment in a way that will enable their children to participate to the best of their ability.

## Challenging discrimination

It is very unlikely that a young child will make a discriminatory remark intentionally and with full understanding of what they are saying. It is more likely to be the case that offensive comments are made innocently as simple observations. Children may point out that others have different colour skin or speak with an accent. These comments can be used as conversation starters about difference. Otherwise, children may inadvertently offend peers by singling them out for some reason and require explanation as to why this might cause offence.

## Challenging negative influences

Of course it is also the case that children may repeat prejudicial remarks and exhibit discriminatory behaviours they have heard and seen elsewhere. Again, it is very unlikely that they will understand the underlying tone and meaning. They are most probably echoing the words and behaviours of others. This can put practitioners in a difficult position because it means confronting the problem by speaking to parents, who may well be the original source. Deal with this in the first instance by taking parents aside for an informal chat. Explain what their child has said or done and ask for their help in explaining why it is inappropriate and offensive. This will deliver the message that you are unwilling to accept this kind of behaviour without being accusatory or apportioning blame. If the behaviour continues invite the parents to a formal meeting with your manager and explain again that it is unacceptable.

If you are concerned that the views expressed by a child, parent or family member are extremist or support a terrorist ideology it becomes a safeguarding issue and you have a legal responsibility to report it.

# Literacy

Help children understand the importance of mutual respect

and tolerance and explain what can happen when prejudice and hatred take hold with the help of the stories below.

## Prejudice and hatred

*Tusk Tusk* by David McKee (Andersen) – this is the story of two groups of elephants, the black and the white, who wage war against each other. The war ends with death and for years elephants disappear off the face of the earth. Many years later a new group of elephants emerges. These grey elephants are the

---

### Think about...

...how you create a cohesive learning community with an ethos that promotes tolerance and inclusion and challenges discriminatory attitudes:

- Do your learning resources and learning environment reflect the diversity of British society?

- How do you ensure children who are learning EAL and their families are fully informed and included?

- How do you ensure children with SEN and their families are catered for?

- Do you take the opportunity to build on children's comments about difference to start a conversation and challenge discriminatory attitudes?

- Do you know how you would deal with a parent or family member who exhibits discriminatory behaviour?

---

# Literacy

| Aspect | Development statement/ Early Learning Goal | How can you use literature to promote mutual respect and tolerance of different faiths and beliefs? |
|---|---|---|
| **Reading** | Listens to stories with increasing attention and recall; describes main story settings, events and principal characters; enjoys an increasing range of books; demonstrates understanding when talking with others about what they have read. | Share stories that explore issues surrounding tolerance, discrimination and prejudice. Use these as a springboard for discussion. Encourage children to consider what happens in these stories and make connections with their own experiences. Share stories that feature characters of different cultures, faiths, races, genders, sexualities and with disabilities. |

- What are good reasons for deciding whether you would like to be friends with someone or not?

- What do you think the grey elephants should do now?

- What do you think will happen to the grey elephants if they start picking on each other for having different sized ears?

Provide large coloured card elephant templates and craft materials. Invite the children to choose an elephant in their favourite colour and decorate it in any way they like. Mount the elephants with the children's names on a large display board with the title, 'We are all different but happy together'.

## Intolerance of difference

*The Ugly Duckling* by Hans Christian Andersen – there are many versions of this traditional tale that tells the story of a little bird who is discriminated against because he does not look like the rest of his family. He is bullied into leaving and hurt by others he approaches as he tries to find his true home. Eventually he is accepted by a family of swans and realises he was a swan all along. Although on the face of it this story appears to deliver the message that we should stick to our own, it actually highlights the potential consequences of discrimination in terms of creating divisions within society.

**Reflecting on the story: Do we all have to be the same?** Use the story to introduce the concept of discrimination and explore the consequences of bullying. Ask the children the following:

- Why were the other animals horrible to the Ugly Duckling?

- How do you think the Ugly Duckling felt?

- Do you think it is right to describe the duckling as 'ugly' just because he looks different?

- What would the world be like if we all looked the same, liked the same things and had the same ideas?

- What happened to the Ugly Duckling in the end?

- Is it right that the duckling had to find a family of birds that looked like him so he could feel happy and comfortable?

- Do we all have to be and look the same to live, work and play together?

Make small individual apple pies to illustrate the point that we are all essentially the same on the inside, although we look different on the outside and have individual personality traits.

- Allow the children to make motifs out of pastry to put on the top of their pies (our bodies look different on the outside).

peace-loving descendants of the warring elephants and wish to live in peace. However, like their ancestors they cannot help but let prejudice creep in and before long there are divisions between the little ears and the big ears. This is an excellent story for exploring what happens to societies when people discriminate against each other and prejudice is allowed to breed.

**Reflecting on the story: Without prejudice** Ask the children to think about what happened between the elephants in the story and encourage them to explore what prejudice means as well as the consequences of prejudicial hatred. Use the following questions to facilitate the discussion:

- Why did the elephants hurt each other?

- Was it okay to hurt each other in the way they did?

- Does having a particular skin colour make a group of elephants bad?

- Can we tell what someone is like simply by looking at them?

- Tell me why you like your friend _____. Would you still like her/him if s/he had smaller ears than you?

- Is it right to decide whether you like someone or not because of their skin colour?

## Mutual respect and tolerance of different faiths and beliefs

- Show the children a couple of eggs that have shells in different shades of colour and point out the difference. Invite the children to crack the eggs open and point out that they have the same contents (our bodies contain the same things inside). Whip up the eggs and use them to brush the tops of the pies.

- When the pies are baked take some time to look at and compare the different pasty toppings then cut them open to reveal the same apple fillings.

- Offer the children a choice of cream, custard or ice-cream to eat with their pies (we all have different personalities).

## Intolerance and discrimination

*The Pirates Next Door* by Jonny Duddle (Templar) – in this story a family of pirates move into a quiet town called Dull-on-Sea much to the dismay of the local residents. Young Matilda thinks the Jolly-Rogers are an exciting prospect and quickly makes friends with their son Jim-Lad. Meanwhile, the town erupts into malicious gossip about the new family and rumours about poor hygiene, rats and bad behaviour start flying around. The town unites and petitions to get rid of the family. Then one day the Jolly-Rogers set sail,

leaving a parting gift of treasure for their inhospitable neighbours, proving that they are not so bad after all. This is an excellent picture book for exploring prejudice, intolerance and discrimination.

**Reflecting on the story: You are not welcome here** Introduce the concepts of intolerance and discrimination by asking the children to think about how the residents of Dull-on-Sea treat the Jolly-Rogers in the story. Try asking the following questions:

- What does Matilda think of Jim-Lad and his family?

- Why do you think she likes Jim-Lad so much?

- Why don't the other town residents like the Jolly-Rogers?

- Do you think what the residents say about the Jolly-Roger family is true?

- Where do you think the residents get these ideas from?

- Why do you think the pirates give the town residents treasure before they leave?

- How do you think the residents feel about the pirates at the end of the book?

## Understanding the world

| Aspect | Development statement/ Early Learning Goal | How does this link to mutual respect and tolerance? | Practice that promotes mutual respect and tolerance of different faiths and beliefs |
| --- | --- | --- | --- |
| **People and communities** | Talks about past and present events in their own lives and in the lives of family members; knows about similarities and differences between themselves and others, and among families, communities and traditions. | Mutual respect and tolerance come with being educated about different cultures, religions and beliefs. | Inviting children to share their experiences with their friends and peers and encouraging them to be proud of their family and where they come from. Celebrating a range of religious and cultural festivals and inviting parents and families to join in. Celebrating the diversity of ethnicities and cultures that comprise the population of Great Britain, for example by learning about multicultural art, literature and food. Introducing children to different languages. |

- How do you think the residents feel about their own behaviour when they discover the gifts?

# Understanding the World

The EYFS ensures children learn out about different cultures, religions and beliefs and the associated traditions and rituals through the people and communities aspect of understanding the world. Promoting mutual respect and tolerance involves exploring the similarities and differences between people and communities and thinking about what it means to be British as part of the diverse society that Great Britain encompasses.

# Tolerance, respect and understanding

Prejudice stems from fear and ignorance. Tolerance, respect and understanding come with education. It is therefore vital that young children are educated about a range of cultures, religions and beliefs so they grow up understanding and respecting difference instead of fearing it.

## Festivals

Religious and cultural festivals offer plenty of age-appropriate ways to introduce different cultures, faiths and beliefs to young children:

- Find out if your local authority or nearby libraries and museums loan out resource boxes containing artefacts from different religions.

- Source stories linked to world religions to share (see resources).

- Play traditional games linked to each particular festival.

- Prepare traditional foods that are eaten as part of the celebrations.

- Make decorations and cards.

- Decorate the home corner to reflect different festival celebrations.

- Carry out art and craft projects; make objects and create pictures that are linked to different religions and festivals, for example Diwali diva lamps, Easter nests and Chinese New Year lanterns.

- Invite children to bring in photos from their family and community celebrations to share with the other children in the group. Parents or guardians could be also invited in the setting to share experiences with the children.

- Organise parties and invite families to come in and celebrate festivals together.

Ask parents if they can help with any of these activities. They may be able to bring food in for the children to try. They might like to bring in some music, teach the children some games or tell them a story.

## Collective worship

Under section 70 of the School Standards and Framework Act 1998 pupils attending maintained schools in England and Wales are required 'on each school day' to 'take part in an act of collective worship'. This includes reception classes but not nursery. Schedule 20 of the Act states these acts of worship must be 'wholly or mainly of a broadly Christian character'.

However, it explains as long as the majority of acts of worship during a school term are of Christian character the remainder need not be. It further states, 'When determining the character of the collective worship which is appropriate' schools must consider 'any circumstances relating to the family backgrounds of the pupils'. The requirement to carry out collective worship can be assimilated with the requirement to promote British values:

- Remember just under half of your acts of collective worship can reflect religions other than Christianity. Take this as an opportunity to introduce other religions and beliefs to the children, even if you have no other religions represented in your current intake.

- Plan collective worship that represents the faiths of all the children in your class.

- Compare the teachings of different religions and beliefs to highlight similarities between moral messages.

- Invite local religious leaders of different faiths to come and lead acts of collective worship.

- Visit local places of worship to find out more about different religious practices. This is an especially valuable experience for children who live and go to school in an area that is predominantly populated by people of the same ethnicity, culture and religion. Take the children out to experience different ways of life.

- Remember many families are non-religious and it is possible to teach spiritual, moral, social and cultural development without the use of a religious text.

- Think about posing a thought for the day like BBC Radio 4 and similarly represent thoughts from a range of different religious and humanist teachings.

- If collective worship is carried out during assembly time, it is a good idea to keep the teaching of spiritual, moral, social and cultural development separate from religious worship. This will ensure children who are withdrawn from collective worship by parents do not miss out (BHA, 2016).

## Personal experiences

Often the best opportunities to explore and challenge attitudes towards difference spring from conversations with the children. Listen out for comments that present an opportunity to challenge perceptions and champion difference.

# Appreciation and celebration

Use food, art and literature to help children appreciate the vibrancy of life that multiculturalism brings (there are links with expressive arts and design here):

- Offer children a wide variety of foods from different cultures at snack time. Talk about the flavours and smells and ask the children to explain why they like or dislike certain foods and flavours.

- Invite parents in to prepare traditional dishes with the children. Talk about the different ingredients and where they come from. Find out what kind of climates the ingredients are grown and prepared in.

- Visit specialist supermarkets that sell foods from other countries. Talk about the sights, smells and tastes. Allow the children to choose and buy some products to take back to the setting and taste.

- Set up a role play spice market with real spices from different countries.

- Mix spices with drops of water and paint with them.

- Find out where the different foods available in British supermarkets are exported from and how the British diet is influenced by other dietary cultures.

- Play background music that represents a range of different cultures. Ask parents to recommend artists and loan you albums.

- Use music from a range of cultures for music and movement sessions.

- Introduce children to instruments from around the world (again you may be able to borrow some examples from your local authority, museums or neighbouring schools).

- Invite multiethnic performers into the setting to workshop with the children.

## Case study: I can marry anyone

Jack (age 5) has just returned to school after a weekend attending the wedding of two close friends of the family:

Jack: My Uncle Ashton and Uncle Michel got married and we went there on a big red bus.

Emily: I'm going to marry Sam.

Carey: Was it your uncles that got married?

Jack: Well, they're not my real uncles but I just call them that.

Carey: But they can't get married. If you're a boy you have to marry a wife. I'm going to have a husband.

Jack: Well I might want to marry a boy. I can marry anyone I like.

Carey: You can't marry a boy, only a girl. Boys can be friends with other boys and girls can be friends with other girls but they can't get married because it has to be a boy and a girl, like a mum and a dad.

Jack: No, serious. They did get married, but they're not dads, they don't have any children.

Emily: It's true. Boys can marry boys and girls can marry girls. But I'm going to marry Sam.

Teacher: Yes, it is true Emily. We can all choose who we would like to marry just like Jack's uncles. I bet you had a wonderful weekend Jack. I do love a good wedding!

The reception teacher in this example allows the children to consider and discuss the issue between themselves before joining in and confirming that same sex marriage is possible. Carey's comments highlight a need to broaden the children's knowledge and understanding of different families and relationships. The teacher takes a mental note to share some stories about same sex parents with the children and source books featuring members of the lesbian, gay, bisexual and transgender (LGBT) community for the book corner (see resources).

- Display multicultural artworks and provide art materials for the children to emulate them.

# The Prevent duty and your Ofsted inspection

## What will Ofsted be looking for?

Ofsted recently introduced three new inspection documents, which make it clear that early years providers should be able to produce evidence that they have robust safeguarding procedures in place and are actively promoting British values within their settings.

Inspecting Safeguarding in the Early Years, Education and Skills Settings states **inspectors will be looking for evidence that practitioners have a 'clear approach to implementing the Prevent duty'** (Ofsted, 2015b p.11). The Common Inspection Framework explains when making judgements about the effectiveness of leadership and management inspectors will evaluate **'the extent to which leaders, managers and governors actively promote British values'** as defined in the Prevent strategy (Ofsted, 2015a, p.13). These two documents should be read in conjunction with The Early Years Inspection Handbook (Ofsted, 2015c), which provides useful grade descriptors to help exemplify.

In order to achieve outstanding for the effectiveness of leadership and management in relation to the Prevent duty a setting must meet statutory safeguarding requirements and **'have created a culture of vigilance'** where children are listened to, staff are trained to identify and report concerns, and work with other agencies is effective. It must also demonstrate that, **'the promotion of equality, diversity and British values is at the heart of the setting's work... including tackling any instances of discrimination and being alert to potential risks from radicalisation and extremism'** (Ofsted, 2015c, p.34).

To achieve outstanding for teaching, learning and assessment a setting must **'provide an exceptional range of resources and activities that reflect and value the diversity of children's experiences'**, and **'actively challenge gender, cultural and racial stereotyping and help children gain an understanding of people, families and communities beyond their immediate experience'** (Ofsted, 2015c, p.38).

# The Prevent duty and your Ofsted inspection

Furthermore, to achieve outstanding for personal development, behaviour and welfare there must be **'vigilant and highly consistent implementation of robust policies, procedures and practice'** (Ofsted, 2015c, p.41). Settings must 'teach children the language of feelings and give them opportunities to reflect on their differences' so they **'develop a positive sense of themselves and their place in the world'** and **'demonstrate exceptionally positive behaviour and high levels of self-control, cooperation and respect for others'** (Ofsted, 2015c, pp.41-42).

A setting will be judged as inadequate if **'breaches of the statutory requirements for safeguarding and welfare** and/or learning development have a significant impact on children's safety, well-being and personal development', 'children have a **narrow experience that does not promote their understanding of people and communities** beyond their own or help them to recognise

and accept each others' differences', and **'equality, diversity and British values are not actively promoted in practice'** (Ofsted, 2015c, pp.35-43).

What's more, 'early education funding regulations in England have been amended to ensure providers who fail to promote' British values will **'not receive funding from local authorities for the free early years entitlement'** (HM Government, 2015a, p.12).

## How will Ofsted collect evidence?

Inspectors will want to see that robust safeguarding procedures are in place and the promotion of British values is embedded within your setting's culture through everyday practice.

## Prevent and your Ofsted inspection

| What will inspectors do? | What are they looking for? |
| --- | --- |
| Observe and talk to the children | Evidence of a safe, inclusive learning environment with a strong focus on spiritual, moral, social and cultural development. **Children will demonstrate this if they are in a learning environment where they are comfortable and feel confident to voice their opinions. They will play with or alongside others and demonstrate inclusive behaviour and tolerant attitudes.**<br><br>Where this is not the case inspectors will want to see evidence that children are being taught to regulate their own behaviour in terms of how they function within the setting, manage their feelings and relate to others. **This means ensuring staff intervene, challenge and guide children who express discriminatory views or behaviour that is contrary to British values.** |
| Look at planning to see what type of educational programme the children are receiving | Evidence that children are experiencing a well-balanced curriculum that enables them to develop an understanding of a range of ethnicities, cultures and beliefs, and actively promotes British values. **This means planning activities that introduce children to and help them develop a broad knowledge and understanding of a range of issues.**<br><br>Evidence that personal, social and emotional development is recognised as a prime area of learning. Children taking part in activities that aim to help them develop a positive sense of self, teach them to respect others and enable them to learn right from wrong. **Again, this means specifically planning activities to develop the children's personal and social skills.** |
| Look at assessment records to see if children's progress (or lack of) is being monitored and any necessary intervention is in place | Evidence that staff have high expectations of all children regardless of their ethnic, cultural or religious background.<br><br>Evidence that leaders, managers and their staff have identified gaps in achievement between different groups of children and are taking steps to narrow these gaps. **This means ensuring observation records include space for assessment notes and next steps. In addition, a cohort progress tracker that allows analysis of the children's overall progress should be used to highlight any differences between different groups of children. Barber and Paul-Smith (2010) provide a good example.**<br><br>Evidence that staff consider information from parents and children when making assessments. **This means ensuring assessment records include notes and observations from parents and comments from children.**<br><br>Furthermore, **PACEY (2015) highlights the importance of explaining how the pupil premium is to be used to boost the achievement of disadvantaged children.** |

| What will inspectors do? | What are they looking for? |
|---|---|
| Look at the physical environment and assess how well it supports learning | Evidence that learning resources, equipment, displays and images reflect diversity. **This should not be a token effort. It is not enough to place multicultural resources strategically around the setting. Such resources should feature in planning and be used to enhance learning.**<br><br>That labelling and visual material displayed around the setting is accessible to all, e.g. translated into relevant languages. |
| Carry out joint observations with the lead practitioner or manager to evaluate a lesson or activity | Whether leaders and managers effectively evaluate practice and how well they feed back to and support staff to make improvements. **This means demonstrating an awareness of whether staff behave as positive role models, i.e. treating all children equally, respecting their views and opinions and demonstrating a positive attitude toward different cultures and beliefs.**<br><br>**Furthermore, it means being aware of the need for staff to listen to children, offer considered responses and engage them in dialogue which encourages them to consider alternative viewpoints.** |
| Talk to the provider, manager or childminder to evaluate leadership and management | Evidence that leaders and managers understand the need to ensure their staff receive training in safeguarding and the Prevent duty, as well as the importance of actively promoting British values. **This means arranging such training, either in the form of INSET, via the local authority or online.** |
| Talk to staff | Evidence that staff know and understand the indicators that may suggest a child is at risk of radicalisation and are aware of any risks associated with children being exposed to extremist views. This includes having an understanding of the potential risk in the local area. **This means ensuring staff are trained to enable them to identify possible risks and signs.**<br><br>Evidence that staff understand safeguarding procedures and are aware of all supporting policies that are in place. **This means ensuring staff have received safeguarding and Prevent training and feel confident about what to do if they have any concerns.**<br><br>Evidence that staff identify with and are promoting the fundamental British values of democracy, rule of law, individual liberty, and mutual respect and tolerance of different faiths and beliefs. |
| Talk to parents | Evidence that all parents and families feel valued, supported, consulted and included by the setting and are confident about the welfare of their children. **This means forging positive relationships with all parents by making them feel welcome and involved in the life of the setting.** Sargent (2013) provides plenty of practical ideas for how to make this happen. |
| Look at and take samples from policies | **Child Protection policy:** That the Prevent duty is included. The policy should identify exposure to extremist views and radicalisation as a potential risk to the welfare of a child. It should also set out the roles and responsibilities of management and staff, procedures for tackling any issues that arise, referral procedures and details of who to contact.<br><br>**Equality, Diversity and Inclusion policy:** That this demonstrates the aim to ensure all children are valued and included irrespective of cultural background, ethnicity and religious belief. There should be a clear intention to eliminate discrimination and foster good relations both within the setting and the local community.<br><br>**English as an Additional Language (EAL) policy:** That this demonstrates the aim to ensure the setting meets the full range of needs of children learning EAL, including valuing their cultural identity and championing the continued use of their first language by highlighting the importance of their linguistic heritage. Sargent (2016) provides an exemplar EAL policy.<br><br>**E-Safety and E-Learning policy:** That this demonstrates an awareness of the potential risks associated with internet use in terms of children viewing inappropriate material and being approached online. It should set out how the setting intends to monitor children's use of ICT equipment that gives them access to the internet and how children will be taught about keeping themselves safe online.<br><br>Evidence that providers have consulted with parents about policies and procedures. **This means asking parents for their views and taking these into account when writing and implementing policies.** |

## Prevent and your Ofsted inspection

| What will inspectors do? | What are they looking for? |
| --- | --- |
| Evaluate the effectiveness of safeguarding procedures | Evidence that leaders and managers have referred to government guidance to ensure safeguarding arrangements meet statutory requirements, promote the children's welfare and prevent radicalisation and extremism. **This means reading the Prevent Duty Guidance (HM Government, 2015a and 2015b), Inspecting Safeguarding in Early Years Education and Skills Settings (Ofsted, 2015a), The Common Inspection Framework (Ofsted, 2015b) and The Early Years Inspection Handbook (Ofsted, 2015c) and using these to inform policies and procedures.**<br><br>That policies are readily available to staff and that staff have a clear understanding of safeguarding procedures. **This means having clear safeguarding procedures and ensuring all staff understand what to look for, when to make a referral and who to refer to.**<br><br>Evidence that staff understand their Prevent duty. **Again, this means ensuring staff have read the relevant policies and have access to Prevent training.** |
| Look at self-evaluation forms and plans for improvement | Completed self-evaluation forms and evidence that these are being used to inform improvement plans. **This means leaders and managers should have an accurate understanding of the setting's strengths and weaknesses, have identified areas for improvement, and have set out the next steps to take to make such improvements.** |
| Look at working partnerships with other agencies and professionals | Evidence that work with partner agencies is effective. **This means having effective arrangements for sharing information and working in partnership with other agencies.** |

# Fulfilling the Prevent duty checklist

- Have you and your staff received child protection and safeguarding training?
  - Are you alert to any potential child protection and safeguarding issues in the children's lives, both in the home and elsewhere?

- Have you and your staff received Prevent training?
  - Are you able to confidently identify children who are at risk of being exposed to a terrorist ideology?
  - Do you have a good understanding of the potential risk of children being exposed to extremist ideas in your local area?

- Are your policies up to date?
  - Does your child protection policy include a section about the Prevent duty?
  - Do you have an equality, diversity and inclusion policy?
  - Does your EAL policy reflect an aim to respect cultural diversity?
  - Does your e-safey and e-learning policy cover the risk of exposure to extremist views online?

- Do you have a designated safeguarding lead and are all staff clear about safeguarding procedures?

- Do you and your staff know what to do if you have concerns that a child in your care is being exposed to extremist ideas?
  - Are you aware of the policies and procedures of the Local Safeguarding Children Board (England), Local Service Board (Wales) or Child Protection Committee (Scotland)?
  - Do you know who to refer to?

- Do you and your staff challenge extremist and discriminatory ideas?

- Are you confident that you are providing a safe and secure learning environment where all children are valued and diversity is celebrated?

- Are children adequately supervised when using computers and internet enabled tablets in the setting?
  - Do you have the necessary filters in place to ensure they are unable to view inappropriate content?

- Do you promote the fundamental British values of democracy, rule of law, individual liberty, and mutual respect and tolerance for those with different faiths and beliefs throughout your everyday practice?

# Resources

## Democracy

- *The Election* by Eleanor Levenson and Marek Jagucki (Fisherton Press)
- *This is Our House* by Michael Rosen (Walker Books)
- *Mine!* by Rachel Bright (Puffin)
- *Elephant Learns to Share* by Sue Graves and Trevor Dunton (Franklin Watts)
- *The Gigantic Turnip* by Aleksei Tolstoy and Niamh Sharkey (Barefoot Books)
- *Never Too Young: How Young Children Can Take Responsibility and Make Decisions* by Judy Miller (Save the Children)
- *Starting With Choice: Inclusive Strategies for Consulting Young Children* by Mary Dickins, Sue Emerson and Pat Gordon-Smith (Save the Children)
- *I Have the Right to be a Child* by Alain Serres, Aurelia Fronty and Sarah Ardizzone (Phoenix Yard Books)
- *The Little Book of Team Games* by Simon MacDonald (Featherstone)

## Rule of law

- *Golden Rules Animal Stories* by Donna Luck and Juliet Doyle (Positive Press)
- *Captain Buckleboots* on the Naughty Step by Mark Sperring and Tom McLaughlin (Puffin)
- *Know and Follow Rules and Understand and Care* by Cheri J Meiners (Free Spirit Publishing)
- *People Who Help Us: Police Officer* by Amanda Askew and Andrew Crowson (QED Publishing)
- *Manfred the Baddie* by John Fardell (Quercus Children's Books)
- *Shifty McGifty and Slippery Sam* by Tracey Corderoy and Steven Lenton (Nosy Crow)
- *Gigantosaurus* by Jonny Duddle (Templar)
- *The Little Book of Listening* by Clare Beswick and Sally Featherstone (Featherstone)
- *Speaking and Listening Activities for the Early Years* \ by Debbie Chalmers (Brilliant Publications)
- *50 Fantastic Ideas for Exploring Emotions* by Sally and Phill Featherstone (Featherstone)
- *Exploring Emotions* by Ros Bayley and Lynn Broadbent (Lawrence Educational)
- *Emotional Literacy in the Early Years* by Christine Bruce (Sage Publications)
- Emotions Stones (www.yellow-door.net)
- Crime scene tape (www.ebay.co.uk)

## Individual liberty

- *Giraffes Can't Dance* by Giles Andreae and Guy Parker-Rees (Orchard Books)
- *I am Henry Finch* by Alexis Deacon and Viviane Schwarz (Walker Books)
- *Blue Chameleon* by Emily Gravett (Macmillan)
- *A Great Big Cuddle: Poems for the Very Young* by Michael Rosen (Walker Books)
- *We Are All Born Free* by Amnesty International (Frances Lincoln Children's Books)
- *My Little Book of Big Freedoms* by Chris Riddell (Amnesty International UK)
- *101 Games for Self-Esteem and 101 Activities to Help Children Get on Together* by Jenny Mosley and Helen Sonnet (LDA)
- *Circle Time for Young Children* by Jenny Mosley (Routledge)
- *Speaking, Listening and Thinking with Dogum* by Ros Bayley and Peter Scott (Lawrence Educational)
- *Helping Young Children to Listen, Helping Young Children to Concentrate and Helping Young Children to Speak with Confidence* by Ros Bayley, Lynn Broadbent and Adrina Flinders (Lawrence Educational)

## Mutual respect and tolerance

- *Whoever You Are* by Mem Fox and Leslie Staub (Harcourt Children's Books)
- *My World, Your World* by Melanie Walsh (Corgi Children's)
- *It's Okay to Be Different* by Todd Parr (Little Brown)
- *The Rainbow Fish* by Marcus Pfister (North-South Books)
- *King & King* by Linda De Haan and Stern Nijland (Tricycle Press)
- *This is My Family: A First Look at Same-Sex Parents* by Pat Thomas (Barron's Educational)
- *My Princess Boy* by Cheryl Kilodavis and Suzanne DeSimone (Aladdin)
- *Rama and Sita* by Malachy Doyle and Christopher Corr (A&C Black)
- *The Story of Hanukkah* by David A Adler (Holiday House)
- *Under the Ramadan Moon* by Sylvia Whitman and Sue Williams (Albert Whitman & Company)
- *The Easter Story* by Heather Amery and Norman Young (Usborne Bible Tales)
- *Everyone Matters: A First Look at Respect for Others* by Pat Thomas and Lesley Harker (Barron's Educational Series)
- *50 Fantastic Ideas for Celebrations and Festivals* by Alistair Bryce-Clegg (Featherstone)

# Resources

- Multicultural Resources for Early Years Education
  www.little-linguist.co.uk/multicultural-resources-for-
  children.html
- Festival Enhancements for 3-7yrs
  http://earlyexcellence.com/product-category/indoor-
  enhancements-3-7-years/festival-enhancements-3-7yrs/

## Internet safety

- *Chicken Clicking* by Jeanne Willis and Tony Ross
  (Andersen Press)

## Further reading

- *Common Inspection Framework, British Values and You*
  by the Professional Association for Childcare and Early
  Years (PACEY)
- *British Values in Early Years Settings & Play Services*
  by Chrissy Meleady. To order a copy contact
  equalitiesmatter@gmail.com
- *British Values in Your Early Years Setting factsheet* by
  National Day Nurseries Association. To order a copy
  go to: www.ndna.org.uk/NDNA/Shop/Factsheets_
  page_1.aspx

# References

4Children (2016) *Fundamental British Values in the Early Years*. Foundation Years. London, 4Children. Available from: www.foundationyears.org.uk/files/2015/03/Fundamental_British_Values.pdf

Barber, J and Paul-Smith S (2010) *Early Years Observation and Planning in Practice*. London, Practical Pre-School Books.

BRIC (2016) *Young Children, Public Spaces and Democracy: The BRIC Project*. Available from: www.bricproject.org/bric-the-project

British Humanist Association (2016) *Collective Worship and School Assemblies: Your Rights*. London, BHA. Available from: https://humanism.org.uk/education/parents/collective-worship-and-school-assemblies-your-rights/

Charlesworth, V (2009) *Critical Skills in the Early Years*. Stafford, Network Continuum Education.

*Counter-Terrorism and Security Act 2015, Chapter 6*. London, TSO. Available from: www.legislation.gov.uk/ukpga/2015/6/section/26/enacted

Department for Education (DfE) (2014a) *Statutory Framework for the Early Years Foundation Stage*. London, TSO.

Department for Education (DfE) (2014b) *Promoting Fundamental British Values as Part of SMSC in Schools: Departmental Advice for Maintained Schools*. London, TSO.

Department for Education (DfE) (2015a) *Keeping Children Safe in Education: Statutory guidance for schools and colleges*. London, TSO.

Department for Education (DFE) (2015b) *The Prevent Duty: Departmental Advice for Schools and Childcare Providers*. London, TSO.

Department for Education and Skills (DfES) (2015) *Curriculum for Wales: Foundation Phase Framework (Revised)*. London, TSO.

Early Education (2012) *Development Matters in the Early Years Foundation Stage*. London, TSO.

Education and Inspections Act 2006, Chapter 40. London TSO. Available from: www.legislation.gov.uk/ukpga/2006/40/contents

Education Scotland (2016) The purpose of the curriculum. *Education Scotland: Learning and teaching. Edinburgh,*

*Education Scotland*. Available from: www.educationscotland.gov.uk/learningandteaching/thecurriculum/whatiscurriculumforexcellence/thepurposeofthecurriculum/index.asp

Goddard, C (2016) All about... British values. *Nursery World*, 8-21 February, pp.25-28.

Gouldsboro, J (2015) *Promoting British values in early years settings*. Early Years Educator, Vol 17, No 6, October, pp.47-52.

HM Government (2011) *Prevent Strategy*. London, TSO.

HM Government (2012) *Channel: Vulnerability Assessment Framework*. London, TSO.

HM Government (2015a) *Revised Prevent Duty Guidance for England and Wales*. London, TSO.

HM Government (2015b) *Working Together to Safeguard Children: A guide to inter-agency working to safeguard and promote the welfare of children*. London, TSO.

HM Government (2015c) *What to do if You're Worried a Child is Being Abused: Advice for Practitioners*. London, TSO.

HM Government (2015d) *Information Sharing: Advice for Practitioners Providing Safeguarding Services to Children, Young People, Parents and Carers*. London, TSO.

HM Government (2015e) *Channel Duty Guidance: Protecting Vulnerable People from Being Drawn into Terrorism*. London, TSO.

HM Government (2015f) *Revised Prevent Duty Guidance for Scotland*. London, TSO.

Holland, P (2003) *We Don't Play with Guns Here: War, weapon and superhero play in the early years*. Berkshire, Open University Press.

*Human Rights Act 1998, Chapter 42*. London, TSO. Available from: www.legislation.gov.uk/ukpga/1998/42/contents

Magnavacchi, L and Wilenski, D (2015) *The Revolutionary Baby: An adventure in two year olds' story-making*. Onreflection Publishing, Sussex. Available from: www.onreflectionpublishing.co.uk

# References

Ofsted (2015a) *The Common Inspection Framework: Education, Skills and Early Years*. London, TSO.

Ofsted (2015b) *Inspecting Safeguarding in Early Years, Education and Skills Settings*. London, TSO.

Ofsted (2015c) *The Early Years Inspection Handbook*. London, TSO.

Professional Association for Childcare and Early Years (PACEY) (2015) *Common Inspection Framework, British Values and You*. Kent, PACEY Commercial Services Limited.

Rosen, M (2014) Dear Mr Gove: what's so 'British' about your 'British values'? *The Guardian*, 1st July. Available from: www.theguardian.com/education/2014/jul/01/gove-what-is-so-british-your-british-values

Sargent, M (2011) *The Project Approach in Early Years Provision*. London, Practical Pre-School Books.

Sargent, M (2013) *50 Fantastic Ideas for Involving Parents*. London, Featherstone.

Sargent, M (2016) *100 Ideas for Early Years Practitioners: Supporting EAL Learners*. London, Bloomsbury.

*School Standards and Framework Act 1998, Chapter 31*. London, TSO. Available from: www.legislation.gov.uk/ukpga/1998/31/section/70

Siraj-Blatchford, I and Sylva, K et al (2004) *The Effective Provision of Pre-School Education (EPPE) Project: Final Report*. London, DfES and Institute of Education, University of London.

UNICEF (2016) *United Nations Convention on the Rights of the Child: Children's Rights and Responsibilities*. New York, Unicef Publications. Available from: www.unicef.org/rightsite/files/rights_leaflet.pdf

United Nations (UN) (1989) *United Nations Convention on the Rights of the Child (UNCRC)*. Geneva, United Nations. Available from: www.ohchr.org/en/professionalinterest/pages/crc.aspx

Welsh Government (2015) *Keeping Learners Safe: The role of local authorities, governing bodies and proprietors of independent schools under the Education Act 2002*. Guidance document no. 158/2015. London, TSO.

# Notes